DATE DUE

DEMCO 38-296

GREAT WRITERS OF THE ENGLISH LANGUAGE

Early Modern Novelists

[S]TAFF CREDITS

Executive Editor
Reg Wright

Series Editor
Sue Lyon

Editors
Jude Welton
Sylvia Goulding

Deputy Editors
Alice Peebles
Theresa Donaghey

Features Editors
Geraldine McCaughrean
Emma Foa
Ian Chilvers

Art Editors
Kate Sprawson
Jonathan Alden
Helen James

Designers
Simon Wilder
Frank Landamore

Senior Picture Researchers
Julia Hanson
Vanessa Fletcher
Georgina Barker

Picture Clerk
Vanessa Cawley

Production Controllers
Judy Binning
Tom Helsby

Editorial Secretaries
Fiona Bowser
Sylvia Osborne

Managing Editor
Alan Ross

Editorial Consultant
Maggi McCormick

Publishing Manager
Robert Paulley

Reference Edition Published 1989
Published by Marshall Cavendish Corporation
147 West Merrick Road
Freeport, Long Island
N.Y. 11520

Typeset by Litho Link Ltd., Welshpool
Printed and Bound in Italy by
L.E.G.O. S.p.a. Vicenza

All rights reserved. No part of this book may be
reproduced or utilized in any form or by any means
electronic or mechanical including photocopying,
recording, or by an information storage and retrieval
system, without permission from the copyright holder.

©Marshall Cavendish Limited MCMLXXXVII
MCMLXXXIX

LIBRARY OF CONGRESS
Library of Congress Cataloging-in-Publication Data
Great Writers of the English Language
    p. cm.
    Includes index vol.
    ISBN 1-85435-000-5 (set): $399.95
    1. English literature — History and criticism. 2. English
literature — Stories, plots, etc. 3. American literature — History
and criticism. 4. American literature — Stories, plots, etc.
    5. Authors. English — Biography. 6. Authors. American — Biography.
I. Marshall Cavendish Corporation.
    PR85.G66 1989
    820'.9 – dc19   88-21077
                                                               CIP

    ISBN 1–85435–000–5 (set)
    ISBN 1–85435–005–6 (vol)

GREAT WRITERS OF THE ENGLISH LANGUAGE

Early Modern Novelists

Henry James

H. G. Wells

W. Somerset Maugham

John Galsworthy

MARSHALL CAVENDISH · NEW YORK · TORONTO · LONDON · SYDNEY

CONTENTS

HENRY JAMES

The Writer's Life 6
A Quiet American
Reader's Guide 12
THE PORTRAIT OF A LADY
The Writer at Work 18
The Master Craftsman
Sources & Inspiration 24
Voluntary Exiles

H. G. WELLS

The Writer's Life 30
Lusty Ambitions
Reader's Guide 36
THE WAR OF THE WORLDS
The Writer at Work 42
Time-Traveller
Sources & Inspiration 48
The Dawn of Science Fiction

W. SOMERSET MAUGHAM

The Writer's Life 54
Exiled in Splendour
Reader's Guide 60
OF HUMAN BONDAGE
The Writer at Work 66
'Teeming Memories'
Sources & Inspiration 72
Secret Agents

JOHN GALSWORTHY

The Writer's Life 78
Man of Principle
Reader's Guide 84
THE FORSYTE SAGA
The Writer at Work 90
A Voice for Freedom
Sources & Inspiration 96
The Theatre of Ideas

BIBLIOGRAPHY 101

INDEX 102

HENRY JAMES

1843 - 1916

American by birth, Henry James chose to adopt England as his
home. England in turn adopted him as a literary celebrity – he
enjoyed the admiration and even the adoration of Europe's greatest
artistic figures. But the strength of James' work is that it derives from
his rootlessness – from his knowledge of the cultural divide between
American and European minds and manners. It was a divide which
cleft James' own life. His triumph is that he rose above it
to arrive at his wonderfully shrewd understanding of human nature.

A Quiet American

Henry James sailed to Europe in search of a 'culture' and 'civilization' that formed a sharp contrast with his American background. The experience turned him into 'that queer monster, the artist'.

Henry James led a long, brilliantly productive life. Drawn from America to Europe, he counted among his friends the French novelist, Gustave Flaubert, and the English writers J. M. Barrie and Hugh Walpole. Although he never achieved any major financial success, his talents as a writer were legion and unquestioned. As his biographer Leon Edel was to write, with Henry James 'the American novel, in a single leap, attained a precocious maturity it has never surpassed.'

Born on 15 April 1843, in New York, Henry James was the second of five children. His father, Henry James senior, was a celebrated religious philosopher, his mother Mary the 'protecting spirit' of the family. Young Henry's early years were spent on the move; his father wanted the broadest and best education for his children, and Europe seemed to hold the key. So, when Henry was just six months old the family sailed to England, and by the time the future novelist was 17 he had lived in London, Paris, Geneva, Boulogne and Bonn, as well as New York City and Albany in the United States.

Even as a boy, therefore, James never had a chance to put down roots or to consider himself a born-and-bred native of any country. Later, when he was to remember his earliest years, James wrote, 'I often . . . wonder if I was really as little appreciated as I fully remember feeling at that time . . . at a very early age the problems of life began to press upon me in such an unnatural way and I developed such an ability for feeling hurt and wounded that I became quite convinced by the time I was twelve years old that I was a foundling.' This sense of not belonging faded with the years but never completely left him.

THE END OF YOUTH

James began to write in secret at the age of 17, and when in 1864 he and his family moved to Boston, he was welcomed by the editors of two literary magazines as a promising young writer. James made his literary debut the following year with a story published in the *Atlantic Monthly*.

It was not until James was 26 that he made his first real break from his family, sailing for Europe and renewing his love of London. He stayed in that 'dreadful, delightful city', writing and meeting such literary idols as George Eliot, until just one year later, when he heard of the death of his cousin Minny Temple. It was she who was to inspire some of his most important fictional heroines and her death marked for him, and for his brother William, 'the end of our youth'.

James returned to the United States and for five years lived mainly in New York, a somewhat 'brooding

'the keystone of the arch'
(right) Henry's mother Mary raised her five children with selfless devotion but with a 'firm rein'. She was the family's security and strength, earning an undying affection as 'our protecting spirit'.

Paternal identity
(below) An eminent philosopher, Henry senior was regarded by his children as ineffectual; 'we all used to brutally jeer at him'. The younger Henry was to use this 1854 daguerreotype as a frontispiece to his autobiography A Small Boy and Others.

G. Caillebotte - Paris, A Rainy Day. Art Institute of Chicago

exile'. Although busy on his first novel, *Watch and Ward*, he was ill at ease, not yet having found his place in the world. Slowly and deliberately, he set about building up his literary career, trying to gain financial independence. By 1875, when he was 32, he felt that he could leave New York ('fatal to the imagination') and support himself in Europe. America for him, as for other novelists of his generation, was 'too thinly composed', lacking the palpable material out of which novels are made.

In Paris, James earned his first regular income as the French correspondent of an American paper, but he eventually resigned when his editor asked for more popular, robust copy. Fortunately his third novel, *The American*, was a financial success.

Although he became friendly with a group of distinguished writers in Paris, including Gustave Flaubert and Ivan Turgenev, James felt that he would be an 'eternal outsider' there. Accordingly he headed for London where within two years he had become such a social success that, in the 1878/9 season, he dined out no fewer than 140 times.

All the while James was writing home telling his parents and sister Alice about his literary and social activities. What was noticeably absent from his letters was any mention of some romantic attachment. James never became involved with any woman, and always

Key Dates

1843 born in New York

1864 family settles in Boston. First story published anonymously

1870 death of Minny Temple

1875 leaves America for Paris, then London

1881 *The Portrait of a Lady* and *Washington Square* published

1882 deaths of mother and father

1886 moves to Kensington. *The Bostonians* published

1898 moves to Rye

1910 deaths of William and Robertson James

1915 becomes a British citizen

1916 awarded Order of Merit. Dies in London

'A Tragical Pilgrimage'
(above) The artistic life of Paris was a lure to the budding writer Henry, and there he befriended Zola, Flaubert and Turgenev before finally 'turning English all over'.

Civil War
(below) An 'obscure hurt' prevented Henry from following his brothers Robertson and Wilky into battle, but he was never to forget the 'flagrant difference' the war made to America.

Peter Newark's Western Americana

maintained that love was a 'deterrent to the full life', by which he meant that he believed it destroyed a man's independence. He did, however, become friendly with the novelist Constance Fenimore Cooper whom he met on a trip to Florence. Constance was rather isolated and lonely, and reached out to this somewhat younger, successful writer. But he responded with mannered politeness, beyond which she could not probe.

In 1881, James returned to the United States, but the trip only confirmed the rightness of his decision to live abroad. Furthermore, he was in Washington when he received news of his mother's critical illness. She died in Cambridge, Massachusetts, the day before he returned. He was devastated. 'It is impossible for me to say – to begin to say – all that has gone down into the grave with her. She was patience, she was wisdom, she was exquisite maternity.'

'ANCHORAGE FOR LIFE'

James was badly depressed but, back in England, tried to continue his writing. It was not long, however, before his father too became seriously ill. Eleven months later, in December, came the second urgent message to return home. Again, James arrived too late – his father had been buried the day before his ship docked. When James reached the family home he found a last, unopened letter to his father from his brother William. James took the letter to the graveside, and slowly read it aloud, believing that 'somewhere out of the depths of the still, bright winter air' his father heard.

But family sadness was not at an end. Though only 36, his sister Alice had been ill for years and when his father's estate was settled, James gave his entire share to her, to ensure her financial security. He then returned once more to Europe, determined to live by his pen.

Guy de Maupassant
(right) Henry admired the celebrated French writer's work, but was appalled by his attitude to women. While Henry was almost a Puritan, his friend was shockingly brazen about his own sexual appetite. When the pair dined together in London in 1886, Maupassant's roving eye lighted on one beautiful woman after another. With characteristic candour, he demanded that Henry 'Go over and get her for me!' When Henry refused each new appeal, the Frenchman declared that his host didn't seem to know anyone in London. Parisians were well aware of Maupassant's reputation (below right), and many agreed with James when he said his friend was 'a Cad – of Genius'.

Boston, Massachusetts
(below) After extensive travels abroad, the James family settled in Boston, a European-style city, in 1864. One year later the Atlantic Monthly published Henry James' first story in his own name.

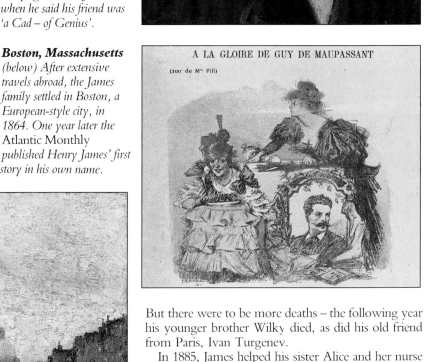

A LA GLOIRE DE GUY DE MAUPASSANT
(200° de Mme Fifi)

But there were to be more deaths – the following year his younger brother Wilky died, as did his old friend from Paris, Ivan Turgenev.

In 1885, James helped his sister Alice and her nurse settle in Bournemouth, and set about finding his own permanent home in London; an 'anchorage for life'. Despite the emotional setbacks of this period he worked on and, by his late 40s, had established a considerable reputation as a novelist. *The Portrait of a Lady*, *Washington Square* and *The Bostonians*, as well as his tales and short stories, had given him the literary success he craved, but little financial reward. So Henry James the novelist now turned to the theatre.

As with his fiction, so with his drama. James made a characteristically quiet and careful entrance into this new world, but his play – the dramatization of his novel *The American* – lasted just 70 nights. The fact that it even ran for that long was mainly due to a visit from the Prince of Wales.

Portrait of Flaubert by Eugene Giraud. Versailles/Lauros-Giraudon

Gustave Flaubert
(left) In 1875, Henry James was introduced to Flaubert, then France's leading writer, by the Russian novelist Turgenev. James found Flaubert 'simple, honest, kindly and touchingly inarticulate'. Though he was initially impressed with French literary circles, he soon found them showy and limited, and began to yearn to be in England.

Notebook sketches
(right) Henry had enjoyed sketching since his days in Newport, and his letters and notebooks contain many of his pencil drawings. During medical treatment at Malvern in 1869, the writer made several sketches of the countryside and houses around Tewkesbury.

her company, and they went on tours of England and France together. Because she took up so much of his work-time, his favourite name for her was the 'Angel of Devastation'. Despite warm personal friendships such as this, he was often extremely lonely.

James' self-contained emotional life was interrupted by three relationships he had with younger men over the next seven years. At the age of 56, he met the sculptor Hendrik Andersen and soon after invited him to spend a few days at Rye. He followed this with a number of intimate letters – the like of which he had never written before – filled with lavish praise, aching loneliness, jealousy and brooding hurt.

In the meantime, James suffered more bereavements. Alice James died of cancer, and two years later Constance Cooper was found dead on the pavement outside her Venice apartment. As Henry was about to leave London for the funeral, he learned that suicide was suspected, and was so repelled by the 'horror and pity' of this that he immediately cancelled the trip. He was clearly worried that his continuing aloofness over the years had been a factor in Constance's suicide. But he did eventually go to Venice where he hunted through her correspondence and removed his letters. Throughout the years he was to safeguard his private life as completely as he could.

On his return to London, James devoted himself to another play, *Guy Domville*, in a last bid for fame and fortune in the theatre. But it was a humiliating failure. Utterly depressed, he seriously questioned his role as an artist – as is evident in his short stories of the time – and was astounded at the gap between his own ideas and those of the public. James believed that the writer should selflessly devote himself to his Art and in an 'age of trash triumphant' he set a high price on style and form. The public, however, did not.

By now James felt the need for a 'calm retreat' outside London and, in 1898, moved into Lamb House, Rye, in Sussex. It was to be his home for the next 14 years. He settled in with his small domestic staff and his many pets, and bought a bicycle to explore the countryside. No matter where James lived, he was surrounded by the famous. Near neighbours included Joseph Conrad, Stephen Crane, Ford Maddox Ford and H. G. Wells who, with his constant stream of guests from London, prevented the retiring James from becoming dangerously isolated.

James' closest and most enduring friendship was with the American author Edith Wharton, one of the most devoted admirers of his work. James delighted in

---

Fact or Fiction

'THE HEROINE OF OUR COMMON SCENE'

The most radiant of Henry James' cousins was Mary 'Minny' Temple. Henry adored her 'ethereal brightness of presence' and her 'splendid shifting sensibility'. Long after her death from consumption in 1870, the writer would devotedly recall her movements, her joyousness and her courage. Minny was immortalized in the creation of James' most memorable heroines, notably Isabel Archer in *The Portrait of a Lady*.

Minny Temple
Henry's adored cousin served as a model for his heroines. After her death he elevated her memory into a 'disengaged and dancing flame of thought'. Only one photograph of her remains and shows her with her hair cropped short due to illness.

Although their friendship was not long-lived, it did prove the reticent novelist was capable of love and that such feelings could be admitted into his fiction, which had previously been dominated more by intellect than passion. Around this time, he marked the lines 'Live all you can' at the start of a Turgenev novel and shaved off his beard – 'A new face for a new century!'

Four years later, Henry met a young Irishman, Jocelyn Persse, and this time the relationship did continue, albeit with only occasional meetings. James rejoiced in Jocelyn's 'exquisite possession of the Art of Life which beats any Art of mine hollow'. James' friends, however, could not understand his attachment to someone whom they regarded as his cultural and intellectual inferior. But despite the disparity of age and interests, the two were to remain devoted to each other.

A PERSONAL CONFLICT

Remarkably, James published his last three and arguably greatest novels, *The Wings of a Dove, The Ambassadors* and *The Golden Bowl* in just two years, from 1902-04. The following year he visited the United States to gather new source material and, more importantly, to visit the graves of his family: 'I seemed to know then why I had come. It made everything right – it made everything priceless.'

When James was 63, he made one last bid to gain financial security, by compiling his collected works. In the meantime, he met the younger novelist Hugh Walpole. Years later Walpole described how he had offered himself to James, and received the distressed reply, 'I can't, I can't'. Walpole also remarked on the conflict between James' 'puritanism' and 'intellectual curiosity'. This relationship soon petered out, as did James' hopes for his latest literary enterprise which yielded a meagre first payment of $211. The depression this caused him led to a nervous breakdown. He finally built a bonfire from more than 40 years' worth of letters and notebooks, and burnt them all, in accordance with his 'law of not leaving personal and private documents at the mercy of any accidents'.

THE END OF AN ERA

In his last years James suffered much and wrote little. In 1910 his younger brother Robertson died. And a few months later his elder brother William, the distinguished philosopher, to whom he had always been closest, died too. In his grief James wrote to Edith Wharton – 'it has cut into me, deep down, even as an absolute mutilation'.

Three years later, 300 of his friends and admirers arranged a collection to mark his 70th birthday. But James, having had word of this, was appalled by such a 'reckless and indiscreet undertaking' and insisted that they took the money back. Although he did not want it broadcast that he had reached a 'fabulous age', he was at least persuaded to accept a real 'golden bowl', and to sit for his portrait. The painting, brilliantly executed by John Singer Sargent, he willed to the National Portrait Gallery.

The following year was clouded by the outbreak of World War 1, 'so hideous and horrible'. For James it symbolized an ultimate rejection. He had devoted his entire adult life and 20 novels, over 100 tales and short

FAILURE AT THE THEATRE

In the 1890s, Henry James tried to make his fortune from the theatre, and pinned his hopes on his play *Guy Domville*. On the first night, before an audience including critics H. G. Wells, Arnold Bennett and G. B. Shaw, the aspiring playwright was brutally jeered; 'for a moment or so, James faced the storm, his round face white above the beard, his mouth opening and shutting [until the manager] snatched him back into the wings'. Henry referred to it as 'the most horrible horror of my life'.

Cartoon by Daumier/Jean-Loup Charmet

BBC Hulton Picture Library

S & O Mathews

Disciple and friend
(left) Edith Wharton was a far more popular (and wealthy) writer than Henry James. But she admired James' work to the point of adoration, and the pair became fast friends. Her ebullience and the distractions of her company – which included the privilege of trips in her car – often annoyed him. Her intrusions into his time led him to refer to her as the 'Angel of Devastation'.

Literary friends

(right) Max Beerbohm captured the intensity of the friendship between Joseph Conrad and Henry James; he shows them conversing at an afternoon party in 1904. Conrad was only one of a literary circle that surrounded James when he moved to Rye. H. G. Wells, Stephen Crane, Rudyard Kipling and Edmund Gosse were all regular visitors.

Lamb House, Rye

(below) James moved into his 'calm retreat' in 1898, and it became his haven for the rest of his life. Kipling had said that in Sussex one could feel history twelve men deep, and the idea had appealed to James. With the exception of the garden-studio, the house has been preserved as it was in James' time.

Ties of brotherhood

(right) Henry (shown beardless) and his older brother William enjoyed a lifelong friendship, spoiled only on occasions by rivalry. Their relationship was mainly supportive. After William died in 1910, Henry accepted an honorary degree from Harvard 'with deference to William's memory'. Henry's autobiographical works are notable for their touching portraits of his family.

stories and five plays to constructing and exploring civilized codes of behaviour, which were now being literally blasted apart. Such were his sympathies that he visited the wounded in hospital and, on one notable occasion, even offered a soldier he chanced upon in the street all the money he had in his pocket. He could not imagine how a soldier could endure 'even for five minutes the stress of carnage.' Ageing and disillusioned, he kept on writing for as long as his health allowed, starting two more novels in 1914.

In 1915, when he was 72, Henry James suffered a stroke; and the next day he had a second attack which paralyzed his left side. He became very confused, and even signed some letters as 'Napoleon'. Gradually, however, he seemed to improve – and there was just time that Christmas for the Prime Minister, Herbert Asquith, to rush his name through the New Year's Honours List. He was awarded the Order of Merit for his services to literature.

On 24 February 1916, James spoke of 'a night of horror and terror'. Three days later, the doctor at last announced 'this is the end', and, at 6.00pm, Henry James died. Although he was formally buried at Chelsea Old Church, his sister-in-law smuggled his ashes back to the United States to bury them, as he had requested, beside his mother and sister. This was the very spot where, 12 years before, the great novelist had stood and cried out 'Basta! Basta!' ('Enough! Enough!')

The newspapers were filled with long and devoted obituaries. His writings, though, soon faded from the public mind. Twenty years later, however, Henry James' works re-emerged and were recognized as the product of a rare and precious mind, that of the first great novelist to explore the Anglo–American divide.

THE PORTRAIT OF A LADY

Through the tragic fate of his spirited young heroine, James explores with compassion and insight the perennial themes of lost innocence and shattered illusions.

No-one took the art of the novel more seriously than Henry James, and there are few more moving and majestic examples of its artistry than *The Portrait of a Lady*. It surveys the conflicting attitudes between male and female and Europe and America, from a specifically 19th-century standpoint, but with an insight that is fundamentally timeless.

James is often thought of as a dry aesthete who is more interested in form than feelings, yet it is hard to imagine a more passionate indictment of domestic tyranny or a more poignant study of disappointed idealism than *The Portrait of a Lady*.

GUIDE TO THE PLOT

The heroine, Isabel Archer, is an intelligent, intense young American, who has been adopted by her aunt, Lydia Touchett. Before she left America for England, Isabel had turned down an offer of marriage from a brash businessman, Caspar Goodwood, who is not a man "weakly to accept defeat" – he will reappear in her life.

At the Touchetts' English country house, Gardencourt, Isabel meets Lydia's husband and their son Ralph. Both men are enchanted by her, and the sickly, intellectual Ralph declares a deep but brotherly interest in Isabel, both for what she is and for what she might do. But although Isabel has "a certain nobleness of imagination", she is also "very liable to the sin of self-esteem . . . she was in the habit of taking for granted, on scanty evidence, that she was right". For this "sin of self-esteem", she will pay dearly.

Isabel soon receives a prestigious proposal from Ralph's friend Lord Warburton, a charming, high-minded nobleman. Yet she remains single-minded in her desire for a "free exploration of life". To her, marriage represents restriction rather than security – "there are other things a woman can do". So she refuses Warburton, who is mortified.

There are two female foils to Isabel, both of whom visit Gardencourt. One is an old friend, Henrietta Stackpole, a bright and breezy journalist, while the other is a new acquaintance, the mysterious Madame Merle.

A grand tour
(right) At first stunned rather than delighted to inherit a fortune, Isabel soon decides "that to be rich was a virtue because it was to be able to do". Like other people of her class and country, she wastes no time in setting off for Paris and the Continent.

Discovering England
(below) Fresh from America, Isabel arrives at her uncle's beautiful country home in "the perfect middle of a splendid summer afternoon". Delighted by her new surroundings and companions, Isabel looks forward to being "as happy as possible" in Europe.

Tissot: Gallery of HMS Calcutta. Tate Gallery, London

Max Lieberman: Garden Scene. Christie's/Bridgeman Art Library

Orchardson: The First Cloud. Tate Gallery, London

A rejected suitor
(above) Despite charm,
wealth and power,
Lord Warburton cannot
persuade Isabel to
marry him. To her it
would mean giving up
the life she aspires to.

**Florentine
encounter**
(right) In Italy, the
"land of promise",
Isabel's thirst for
knowledge and culture
is satisfied, with the aid
of her cousin Ralph's
power of "aesthetic
illumination". And
here too, in "the
beautiful city of
Florence", Isabel meets
the most exquisite
subject of all – Gilbert
Osmond, a man who is
to change her life.

Canella: Piazza Signoria. Cassa di Risparmio/Scala

Henrietta expresses Isabel's American independence of mind in a more extrovert, less
self-conscious way. Her realism contrasts
with Isabel's romanticism, and Henrietta's
nose for gossip is a racy counterpart to Isabel's
genuine intellectual curiosity.

Madame Merle appears at Gardencourt at a
turning-point in Isabel's material cir-

> " **I** *don't wish to be a mere sheep in the flock; I wish to
> choose my fate and know something of human affairs
> beyond what other people think it compatible with
> propriety to tell me.'*"

cumstances. Old Mr Touchett is dying, and
on Ralph's persuasion he decides to leave
Isabel a fortune. There is in the house "a per-
ceptible hush that precedes a crisis". This
refers to Mr Touchett's imminent death, but
also clouds Isabel's first meeting with
Madame Merle. Isabel finds the cultivated,
experienced older woman a "more agreeable
and interesting figure" than anyone she has
ever met. But we are made to feel uneasy
about Madame Merle's very perfection – she
is "too flexible, too useful . . . too ripe and too
final". She is indeed to prove a scheming,
wicked fairy godmother to Isabel.

Now she is provided with a generous inheritance, the world opens up for Isabel. She
travels to Europe where she meets – through
Madame Merle – the suave and sophisticated
Gilbert Osmond, and his sweet, unworldly
daughter Pansy. A connoisseur and collector,
Osmond lives on a hilltop outside Florence,
"like a prince in disguise", with what Isabel
perceives as a fine disdain for the rest of the
world. Isabel is drawn to his 'noble' and aesthetic nature, and marries him against the
advice of her most astute friends, and despite
her own declared "love of liberty". She brings
£70,000 to the marriage.

We meet Isabel again three years later, by
which time "the flower of her youth had not

faded; it only hung more quietly on its stem". She has lost her baby son, and had ample time "to think over Mrs Touchett's theory that Madame Merle had made [arranged] Gilbert Osmond's marriage". Husband and wife live in Rome, in a vast mansion symbolically called the Palazzo Roccanera ('Black Rock'). When Ralph sees Isabel, he ponders on the changes that the years have wrought:

Her light step drew a mass of drapery behind it; her intelligent head sustained a majesty of ornament. The free, keen girl had become quite another person; what he saw was the fine lady who was supposed to represent something. What did Isabel represent? Ralph asked himself; and he could only answer by saying that she represented Gilbert Osmond. 'Good heavens, what a function!' he then woefully exclaimed.

Osmond's deep and overriding love of class and money comes to the fore when Isabel's old suitor Lord Warburton reappears on the scene and shows an interest in Pansy. Madame Merle and Osmond put pressure on Isabel to clinch this dazzling match, and Isabel's sense of disillusionment and degradation reaches a new pitch.

More suffering is in store for her. The Countess Gemini, Osmond's frivolous but good-hearted sister, at last feels compelled to tell Isabel that Madame Merle and Osmond used to be lovers and that Pansy is their daughter. This revelation coincides with news that Ralph is dying at Gardencourt. Isabel's urgent desire to see him is countered by Osmond's veto of such an "indecent" idea.

Friendly advice
(right) Isabel's brisk, good-hearted friend Henrietta Stackpole is ever vigilant about her welfare. She is almost alone in criticizing Isabel's tendency to "live too much in the world of [her] own dreams". On meeting Osmond, Henrietta remarks, with comical candour, " . . . for a nice girl you do attract the most unnatural people". But nothing can pierce the illusions Isabel weaves around Osmond.

Alfred Stevens: The Visit (detail). Sterling & Francine Clark Art Institute

Isabel's marriage and her whole future are at a crisis-point as she sets off for England.

SUBTLE TRAGEDY

The Portrait of a Lady is a romantic tragedy which unfolds through subtle nuances of motive and character. James' starting-point – as he described in his Preface to the novel – was 'a certain young woman affronting her destiny'. Isabel Archer 'affronts' her destiny in both senses of the word – she faces it, but also in a sense abuses it. Having decided upon his 'certain young woman', James' problem was to decide what she would do, and how to dis-

close her character. He reveals Isabel's nature in two ways: by showing how she responds both to other characters, and to the culture and corruption of Europe.

Isabel's admiration and trust are dangerously misplaced. Her very inexperience and idealism make her uniquely vulnerable to the machinations of Madame Merle and Osmond. She is instinctively moral, rather than mercenary and acquisitive, but she pays a high price for scruples.

The poignancy and irony of Isabel's plight deepen as she comes to realize fully the nature of the prison she has walked into. Her oppor-

---

In the Background

UPPER CLASS RADICALISM

Isabel calls Lord Warburton "a great radical", but Henrietta Stackpole sees this as incompatible with his ownership of "about half England". Yet his real, if confused, wish to make the traditional order more humane places him in line with aristocratic reformers like Lord Shaftesbury, who helped to effect important social changes.

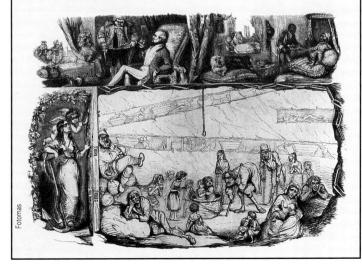

Fotomas

R. Nobili: Cafe Corriello. Gallery of Modern Art, Florence/Scala

tunities for action have always been limited, we are made to feel, simply because she is a woman. Even when she becomes financially independent, her role is more one of adornment than of action – a frustration increased by marriage to a husband who is not slow to tell her "that she has too many ideas and that she must get rid of them".

POETIC IMAGES

James organizes his imagery in the manner of a poet. The claustrophobia gathering around Isabel is evoked by recurrent references to fog, labyrinths, walls and cages. Pervasive images of Nature and flowers stand for the positive forces in the novel, but they are also reminders of fragility and vulnerability. Isabel is a "tight, tender young rose" threatened by Osmond's egotism which lies hidden "like a serpent in a bank of flowers".

Tissot: The Concert (detail). City Art Gallery, Manchester/Edimedia

Isabel's 'evenings'
(left) Now the mistress of an imposing but prison-like Roman palazzo, Isabel sets herself up as a society hostess. Warburton is one of those attracted by her entertainments, and it is here that he meets Pansy Osmond. Beneath the refined conversation and music are played out the tensions arising from Osmond's desire to acquire Warburton as a son-in-law, and Isabel's invidious role as intermediary.

> " *The real offence. . .was her having a mind of her own at all. Her mind was to be his – attached to his own like a small garden-plot to a deer park.*' "

Like a number of James' novels, *The Portrait of a Lady* is about innocence lost. Isabel's trust is callously abused, propelling her into a crisis which is explored in what James considered 'the best thing in the book' – Chapter 42.

Isabel sits by the fire contemplating the horror of her marriage – "the shadows had begun to gather; it was as if Osmond deliberately, almost malignantly, had put the lights out one by one". She goes on to ruefully contemplate the magnitude of her mistake and the abyss of her future – "her soul was haunted with terrors which crowded to the foreground of thought as quickly as a place was made for them". The painful image that especially haunts her consciousness is that of "her husband and Madame Merle unconsciously and familiarly associated".

Rixcall

Bowing to convention
(left) After her marriage, Isabel wakes up to the bitter realization that Osmond's life is just a highly elaborate form: "There were certain things they must do, a certain posture they must take, certain people they must know and not know." Torn between the desire to please and the desire to be herself, Isabel suffers a desperate "sense of darkness and suffocation" as her free and imaginative nature is hemmed in by his "conception of high propriety".

Isabel's traumatic passage from innocence to experience is later confirmed when she sees the ghost that haunts Gardencourt, which Ralph has told her is never seen by a "young, happy innocent person" but only by one who has "suffered greatly".

Isabel has "suffered greatly" because she made a wrong choice. She marries Osmond, thinking him to be noble. He has married her for her money. And Osmond stands in absolute opposition to Isabel's eager and hopeful nature. He has a past as long, dark and dubious as the ruined city he chooses to inhabit.

The enormity of Isabel's mistake is anticipated by Ralph when he speaks out on her enagagement:
"You seemed to me to be soaring far up in the blue – to be sailing in the bright light, over the heads of men. Suddenly some one tosses up a faded rosebud – a missile that should never have reached you – and straight you drop to the ground. It hurts me . . . hurts me as if I had fallen myself!"

Isabel falls far and hard, and in doing so identifies her lot with "the terrible human past" reflected in the ruin of Rome. But in the midst of her disillusionment, she retains a nobility which is the most telling comment on the corrupting forces that cause her fall.

In *The Portrait of a Lady*, it is the two finest characters, Ralph and Isabel, who suffer most. They are both idealistic people who are made to seem incongruous amid the ruthless self-interest of those around them. Yet the loving relationship between the two cousins is the slender thread that keeps Ralph clinging to life, and is the light in Isabel's darkness:

"And remember this," he [Ralph] continued, "that if you've been hated, you've also been loved. Ah but, Isabel – adored!" he just audibly and lingeringly breathed.
This beautiful final scene between Ralph and Isabel sounds a note of redemption that offsets the novel's dominant sense of tragedy.

CHARACTERS IN FOCUS

James describes how the characters in *The Portrait of a Lady* suddenly 'floated into my ken, and all in response to my primary question "Well, what will she *do*?" ' James' characters both fit into, and help to create, the overall design for his heroine's story. His skill in presenting character rests on his power to analyze thought and his mastery of dialogue, each person being given a speech pattern identifiably his or her own. Probably because of this latter quality, James' novels have often been adapted very effectively for the stage.

WHO'S WHO

Isabel Archer A bright young American, brought to England by her aunt, who calls her "'a clever girl, with a strong will and a high temper'".

Lydia Touchett Isabel's aunt, "as honest as a pair of compasses".

Mr Touchett Isabel's uncle, an American banker who has made England his home for the past 30 years.

Ralph Touchett "Ugly, sickly, witty, charming", Isabel's cousin is also her friend and admirer.

Gilbert Osmond An American aesthete living in Italy, whose speciality is "'a great dread of vulgarity'"

Madame Merle An acquaintance of Mrs Touchett, who captivates Isabel with her wit, poise and worldly wisdom. But she is to play an insidious role in Isabel's life.

Caspar Goodwood "A straight young man from Boston" in love with Isabel, who pursues her doggedly in her travels around Europe.

Lord Warburton Ralph's friend, and another of Isabel's suitors – a radical peer "'of excellent ability'".

Henrietta Stackpole Isabel's friend, the intrepid columnist of *The New York Interviewer* – "she went into cages, she flourished lashes, like a spangled lion-tamer". To Isabel she is "proof that a woman might suffice to herself and be happy".

Pansy Osmond Gilbert Osmond's daughter, poised to make her social debut – and a suitable match.

A smooth manipulator, Madame Merle (above) betrays herself by being "too perfectly the social animal". Too late Isabel discovers the truth of her joking admission, "I'm a horror!'"

Ralph Touchett (left), "an apostle of freedom" stands in opposition to Osmond, and in alliance with Isabel, but his illness makes him an impotent, if charming, bystander.

Pansy Osmond (right), the "'little convent-flower'" is her father's most prized possession. Beloved for her other-worldly charm and innocence, she is a pawn in Osmond's deep and worldly game.

"He's the incarnation of taste," *says Ralph of Gilbert Osmond* (below), warning Isabel that if she marries him she will "'be put into a cage'". But Isabel's belief in Osmond's fine nature is virtually an article of faith – until she realizes that he must inevitably take her "way of looking at life . . . as a personal offence", and that their enmity is deep and irreversible.

John William Waterhouse: Portrait of a Young Girl. Fine Art Photographic Library

"Isabel Archer [above] was a young person of many theories" – a mixture of intelligence, romanticism and impressionability. Marriage proposals, no matter how grand, are repugnant to her, for, she says, "'If there's a thing in the world I'm fond of . . . it's my personal independence'". Her aspirations are heroic as well as naive, making her 'fall from grace' all the more intense and shocking. Her marriage to Osmond involves the sacrifice of everything she values most, and she has to face her consequent suffering with a fortitude she could never have imagined. "There were days when the world looked black and she asked herself with some sharpness what it was she was pretending to live for."

A modern man of the New World, Caspar Goodwood (left) is the antithesis of European languor. For him, "Italian trains go at about the rate of an American funeral." Isabel finds his "disagreeably strong push" and "hardness of presence" both stirring and intimidating. But she knows that, for all her fear of his virility, one day "she must make terms with him at least."

P. G. Archainbaud: The Composer. Galerie George/Bridgeman Art Library

THE MASTER CRAFTSMAN

Irritated by the shortcomings of his contemporaries, James sought to bring craftsmanlike precision and polish to the art of writing. With exquisite style, he explored the conflict between the individual and society.

'It is art that *makes* life', wrote Henry James, '. . . and I know of no substitute whatever for the force and beauty of its process.' James was more consciously an artist than any English or American novelist before him. He recognized the inventiveness and vitality of a writer such as Dickens, but deplored the way his books turned into 'fluid puddings', with episodes strung together and many loose ends. Similarly, he criticized Thackeray and Tolstoy for creating 'large loose baggy monsters'. In James' view, the novel ought to be a form of high art, as finely shaped and patterned as a good play or a musical composition.

But although James insisted on the crucial importance of an immaculately polished, stylish approach, he also wished to create a large canvas and make his work a mirror of his time, as Honoré de Balzac had done in his great series of novels 'The Human Comedy'. James found his equivalent of Balzac's all-embracing picture of French society in the 'international' situation – the clash of values that occurred when Americans came into contact with the older, more civilized but often more corrupt culture of Europe.

Yet James' world was in a sense a narrow one: he wrote almost exclusively about people of the higher social classes, who are usually polished, articulate and apparently civilized. Outside the New England artistocracy of the United States though, he found almost nothing to interest him in his native land, claiming that 'It is on manners, customs, usages, habits, forms, upon all these things matured and established, that a novelist lives.'

Nonetheless, 'the Master', as he became known, always probed beneath the façade of manners to explore the way in which human relationships are betrayed for motives of greed, ambition and vanity. The world of Henry James is refined, but there is savagery

Portrait by Burne-Jones. Lamb House/Photo Peter J. Greenhalf

A writing factory
Henry James (left) turned Lamb House into a veritable word-factory, with desks, escritoires and pen-stands situated wherever inspiration might strike, or an idea germinate into a story.

A whorl of words
The satirical cartoon above likened his elaborate sentence structure to the Lady of Shalott weaving her interminable tapestry. (It mirrors Holman Hunt's picture of the entangled lady.)

(Solomon J. Solomon: Conversation Piece. Leighton House, London)

Polite society
The genteel domestic rituals of polite society (left) were meat and drink to James. They supplied all the plots and characters he needed.

Honoré de Balzac
(below left) The great French novelist differed radically from James as writer and man, but James emulated Balzac and considered him 'the master of us all'.

George Eliot
(below) also won James' admiration with her penetrating psychological insight bound up in her excellently crafted literary style.

(Versailles/Bulloz)

(Portrait by L.C. Dickinson. National Portrait Gallery)

stories, but shorter than novels – flourished as a form of serialized fiction in the 19th century. James is a recognized master of the genre.

James' notebooks overflowed with ideas for stories. Sometimes inspiration came without any obvious outside stimulus. For *The Portrait of a Lady*, 'the germ of my idea' was 'the sense of a single character, the character and aspect of a particularly engaging young woman'. Years later, James wrote that 'I seem to myself to have waked up one morning in possession of them – of Ralph Touchett and his parent, of Madame Merle, of Gilbert Osmond and his daughter and sister . . .'

More often, James' imagination was fired by what he called a *donnée* – a 'given' memory or anecdote, heard or overheard in conversation. If the *donnée* was vague or incomplete, so much the better, since that left more scope for the novelist's creative imagination to rework it. *Washington Square*, although it must owe something to Balzac's novel *Eugenie Granet*, originated when the actress Fanny Kemble told James that one of her brothers had jilted an Oxford heiress when he realized that her father would disinherit her if she married him.

The *donnée* for one of James' most famous tales was provided by no less a person than the Archbishop of Canterbury, who had been deeply impressed as a young man by a story that 'would have been thrilling' if he had only been able to find out the details. It concerned 'a couple of small children in an out-of-the-way place, to whom the spirits of certain "bad" servants, dead in the employ of the house, were believed to have appeared with the object of "getting hold" of them'. James put flesh on these bare bones, giving the story a new and ambiguous dimension through the governess-narrator; the result was the classic, controversial, and terrifying ghost story *The Turn of the Screw*.

THE GREAT DICTATOR

Surprisingly, James' working methods, and even his style, were affected by technological changes. During the first part of his career he wrote in longhand, and each of his works was printed straight from the manuscript. In the 1880s, as the typewriter came into common use, James employed a secretarial agency to type up his writings before sending them to the publishers. Then, in 1897, he began to suffer from cramp or rheumatic spasms in his right hand, and rested it by dictating his writing to a secretary.

The experiment was so successful that from this time onwards James dictated all of his fiction. Remarkably, he chose to have his words taken down directly on to the typewriter; he grew so used to the clatter of a given machine that once, when it broke down, he was unable to go on. According to one of his secretaries, Mary Weld, 'He dictated beautifully. He had

behind the refinement. As Prince Amerigo tells his wife Maggie in James' last completed novel, *The Golden Bowl*, "Everything's terrible, *cara* – in the heart of man."

James succeeded in reconciling his artistic ambitions with his need to earn a living. Never a 'popular' writer, he made money because he worked immensely hard, turning his hand to travel books and criticism when he was not creating novels, tales and plays. Many

of his shorter works were 'pot-boilers' written directly for money; among them were two outstanding novels, *The Europeans* and *Washington Square,* which were composed for magazine publication so that James could afford the time to write *The Portrait of a Lady*. Much of his income came from magazines, for which he also wrote no less than 112 long tales, including *The Turn of the Screw* and *The Aspern Papers*. Such 'tales' – longer than short

The Writer at Work

a melodious voice and in some way he seemed to be able to tell if I was falling behind. Typewriting for him was exactly like accompanying a singer on the piano.'

For all its charm, his home at Lamb House was a writing factory; as a small boy, the novelist Compton Mackenzie visited James and noted that the house contained facilities for writing standing up, sitting down and even lying down. James' secretary turned up for work there even on Sunday mornings. To the poet A. C. Benson, James 'admitted that he worked *every* day, dictated every morning, and began a new book the instant the old one was finished.' At other times during the day James researched, read proofs or prepared the next morning's work. Eventually his last secretary, Theodora Bosanquet, was regularly brought back to Lamb House in the evenings for a second working session – during which she was sustained by several bars of chocolate stationed beside the typewriter, with the silver paper thoughtfully removed by James himself, in order to save time.

Dictation encouraged James' tendency to create long, intricate sentences; and this was further reinforced by the ease with which his material could be revised and retyped, if necessary several times. Every revision meant an enrichment and elaboration of the text, in which James strove for increasingly subtle effects and exact observations, piling up qualifying phrases and metaphors. This single sentence from *The Ambassadors* (1903) is typically complex:

The tortuous wall – girdle long since snapped, of the little swollen city, half held in place by careful civic hands – wanders in narrow file between parapets smoothed by peaceful generations, pausing here and there for a dismantled gate or bridged gap, with rises and drops, steps up and steps down, queer twists, queer contacts, peeps into homely streets and under the brows of gables, views of cathedral tower and waterside fields, of huddled English town and ordered English country.

Many readers have found the prose of James' late works, culminating in *The Wings of the Dove, The Ambassadors* and *The Golden Bowl*, practically impenetrable. For them, earlier novels such as *The Portrait of a Lady* and *The Bostonians* are his masterpieces. But the most devoted 'Jamesians', while admitting that his late manner makes considerable demands on the reader, will also insist that it represents his supreme achievement. Both groups would agree that Henry James was one of the greatest artists in the history of the English-language novel.

Lamb House/Photo Peter J. Greenhalf

The view from America
Many of James' books examine the brittle sophistication of Europe in the context of his home country (below).

Theodora Bosanquet
(above) was the last secretary to work at Lamb House. She took dictation directly on to a typewriter.

F. Childe Hassam: Boston Common at Twilight Museum of Fine Arts, Boston

In his long career, Henry James returned again and again to his favourite theme of clashing cultures. Confrontations between American and European culture occur in *The Portrait of a Lady*, *The Europeans* (1878) and *The Ambassadors* (1903). In *The Bostonians* (1886) the clash takes place entirely on American soil – between North and South, between male and female.

James was also preoccupied with the distorting effects of greed and ambition on human relations, exploring them in *Washington Square* (1881) and *The Aspern Papers* (1888). But he was also a master of individual psychology, and his subtle understanding of children's reasoning and perception enlivens a series of fictions including *What Maisie Knew* (1897) and the famous and frightening *Turn of the Screw* (1898). *The Golden Bowl* (1904) closed James' career on a relatively optimistic note: though stoicism and suffering are necessary, civilized values at last triumph over the forces making for disorder. James wrote fascinating prefaces to his novels, explaining their aims and ideas.

THE EUROPEANS
→ 1878 ←

Prosperous, burgeoning provincial 19th-century Boston (left) is the setting for this elegant comedy of manners in which Henry James displays an admirable lightness of touch. The 'Europeans' are Eugenia, Baroness Munster, and her artist brother, Felix; both of them are American-born, but have become steeped in the manners and attitudes of the Old World. Eugenia, the wife of a minor German prince, is about to be set aside for reasons of state, and she and Felix have come to Boston so that she can find a new husband and make their fortunes.

They visit their relatives, the Wentworths, and are established by Mr Wentworth in a house close to his own. Brother and sister are soon enmeshed in the romantic affairs of the family. The light-hearted Felix becomes involved with Gertrude Wentworth, even though Gertrude has an 'understanding' with a local minister, Mr Brand. Mr Brand is loved, in turn, by Gertrude's sister Charlotte. Eugenia attracts an admirer who is rather more sophisticated than the provincial, innocent Wentworths, but she also sets out to fascinate the young and boorish Clifford Wentworth.

James plays off European style against American simplicity with some ironic results – few of the Europeans' plans work out as they expect.

J.D. Bunting: View of Darby, Pennsylvania after the Burning of Lord's Mill. Museum of Fine Arts, Boston

THE AMBASSADORS
→ 1903 ←

The cultural delights of Paris (right) and their impact on provincial, puritanical Americans is the subject of one of James' best-known 'international' books. Lambert Strether, a middle-aged widower, is editor of a literary magazine subsidized by the formidable Mrs Newsome of Woollett, Massachusetts. She despatches Strether to Paris to 'rescue' her son Chad, believing that his inexplicable reluctance to return home must mean he has got himself into trouble. Strether's 'reward' may well be Mrs Newsome's hand in marriage.

But Chad, far from being dragged down by dissolute living, has become an accomplished, self-possessed young man, largely thanks to the influence of a certain Countess de Vionnet. Overwhelmed by the charm of European life, Strether sees things increasingly from Chad's point of view. Mrs Newsome sends new 'ambassadors', who find Strether has changed sides while still being a thoroughly American puritan at heart.

J. Beraud: La Baignoire. Lauros-Giraudon

WHAT MAISIE KNEW
◆ 1897 ◆

Maisie Farange (right), though she lacks the ability to make sense of everything she sees, comes to 'know' a great deal about the way adults behave. When she is six, Beale and Ida Farange are divorced, and a court decrees that Maisie shall spend half the year with one parent, half with the other. Beale and Ida are intent on using Maisie as a vehicle for their mutual loathing, but the little girl takes refuge in silence.

Soon Beale marries Maisie's former governess, Miss Overmore, while Ida finds a husband in the weak young Sir Claude. Both marriages fail. The step-parents become lovers, and Maisie's parents make new conquests of their own. As the sexual roundabout revolves, Maisie finds a friend in a motherly governess, Miss Wix. For a time it seems that the well-meaning Sir Claude will become a true father to her, but the romantic intrigues within the family make this impossible. With the instinct of a survivor, Maisie makes her final choice.

Henry James' child's-eye view of adult entanglements and indiscreet promiscuity makes this book a *tour de force*.

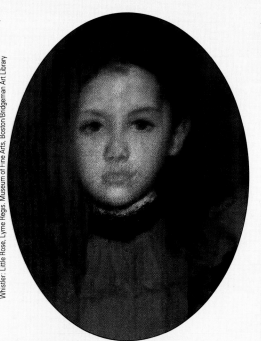

Whistler: Little Rose, Lyme Regis, Museum of Fine Arts, Boston/Bridgeman Art Library

WASHINGTON SQUARE
◆ 1881 ◆

Plain, awkward Catherine Sloper (below) is the heroine of this short, psychological masterpiece. Her father, a cold, unsympathetic physician living on fashionable Washington Square, has made his disappointment in his daughter all too obvious. In his eyes, her only possible attraction to men lies in her inheritance. When handsome Morris Townsend begins paying attentions to her, Dr Sloper's investigations reveal that Townsend is penniless, and he concludes that the young man is a fortune-hunter.

Encouraged by her meddlesome aunt, Catherine accepts Townsend's proposal. But her father threatens to disinherit her, and the marriage is postponed. It is Morris Townsend who is finally worn down by the implacable Doctor. Faced with the prospect of marrying a disinherited Catherine, he reveals his true motives by abandoning her.

Catherine bears up through her personal tragedy, becoming 'an admirable old maid'. After her father's death, Morris Townsend presents himself again, and a final interview between the erstwhile lovers rounds off the story.

Tissot: The Ball. Guillot/Edimedia

Carlton Alfred Smith. Fine Art Photographic Library

THE GOLDEN BOWL
◆ 1904 ◆

The glittering and glamorous lives in this book (left), like the golden bowl bought by Maggie Verver, prove flawed and merely gilded. Adam Verver and his daughter Maggie are devoted to each other. When the time comes for Maggie to marry, she accepts an Italian prince, Amerigo. Adam seeks consolation by marrying Maggie's friend Charlotte, unaware that Amerigo and Charlotte are former lovers parted by want of money. Marriage barely loosens the bond between Maggie and Adam. The Prince and Charlotte, who remain virtual outsiders, resume their old relationship. There are no scenes or separations. Maggie achieves a new maturity and the situation is resolved. Devotees regard this book as James' most profound.

Millais: Just Awake (detail). Perth Museum & Art Gallery

THE TURN OF THE SCREW
◆ 1898 ◆

Eight-year-old Flora (left) and ten-year-old Miles occupy a remote house in Essex. Their governess, the narrator, becomes convinced that the ghosts of a former governess and valet are seeking to take possession of the childrens' souls. More and more incidents suggest it. But there are hints of an alternative explanation: that it is the governess alone who is 'haunted'. At last, determined to save the children, she takes decisive action. This most famous of James' tales proves that terror can be conjured up from quite ordinary incidents – if the reader's own imagination is given enough scope.

Library of Congress/BPCC Aldus Archive

THE BOSTONIANS
◆ 1886 ◆

High-minded women reformers (above) are the butt of James' satire in this story of a battle for the affections and future of a talented young woman. Basil Ransom, a young Southern lawyer, and his cousin Olive Chancellor, an embittered feminist, together attend a suffrage meeting at the home of Miss Birdseye, a kindly, woolly-minded philanthropist. There they hear young Verena Tarrant make a speech. Basil is struck by her beauty, Olive by her potential as a fighter for 'The Cause'. Olive sets about making Verena a suffragist lecturer, while Basil, now in love with Verena, intends to foil her. In the words of one critic, the novel 'affords a mordant and amusing panorama of the near-lunatic fringe of an earnest, intellectual and culturally unfurnished society.'

THE ASPERN PAPERS
◆ 1888 ◆

In a decaying Venetian palazzo (right) lives Miss Bordereau, once mistress of a famous American poet, Jeffrey Aspern. The poet is long since dead, the mistress is now a very old lady. The narrator in this long story is a magazine editor determined to get possession of Aspern's love letters, though Miss Bordereau has consistently refused to publish or reveal their contents. Under an assumed name, the narrator rents an apartment in the palazzo: the old lady needs the money to provide for her spinster niece, Miss Tina. Though Miss Bordereau remains unapproachable, the lonely Miss Tina is more responsive, having put her own interpretations on the attentions paid her by the newcomer. When Miss Bordereau falls ill, the editor's impatience betrays him. He rifles her desk in search of the papers, but is caught and sent packing. A fortnight later he returns and discovers that the old lady has died. Miss Tina welcomes him but makes her expectations clear: she could only ever hand over the letters to a 'relative'. The narrator's response will evidently decide the fate of the Aspern papers.

J. S. Sargent: Interior in Venice (detail). Royal Acedemy, London

Voluntary Exiles

Among the 19th-century stampede of Americans bound for Europe were artists who intended to do more than merely tour the halls of fame. Many intended to win a place there.

When, in *The Portrait of a Lady*, Mrs Touchett speaks of touring Europe with a party of young Americans, she says disparagingly of the race: "they all regard Europe over there as a land of emigration, of rescue, a refuge for their superfluous population."

There was indeed an incessant stream of American tourists invading Europe throughout the 19th century, hungry for history, culture and cheap prices. And among the exodus was a nucleus of artists, their motives ranging from sentimental expectation to frustrated ambition.

Such travellers held the rest in hearty contempt. Henry James came to loathe American tourists abroad, calling them 'vulgar, vulgar, vulgar'. He did not like the grudging pleasure they took in things European. He despised the way Venice was lighted upon by 'the deposed, the defeated, the disenchanted, the wounded, or even only the bored . . . only with the egotism of their grievances and the vanity of their hopes'. James and his kindred American artists meant to sink themselves completely in the European scene – to make homes there and, importantly, to make an impact.

An artistic ambience
American artists found the atmosphere of Paris (right), London and Venice highly conducive to work – charged with new ideas and with reasonably good opportunities to earn a living. The society of local artists and fellow expatriate Americans was at once stimulating and reassuring. At least within the few square miles which comprised the artistic zones, they found an enlightened tolerance that small-town America lacked.

PROSPECT OF PUBLICATION

London, above all, seemed to promise what America could not: bright new ideas, lost traditions, worldly expertise, English airs and graces. For many, living abroad was simply a gesture of distaste for their native country. Lambert Strether, hero of Henry James' *The Ambassadors*, spoke for James when he denounced his home town in Massachusetts as having "only two types of people – male and female – who offer opinions on only three or four subjects." Edgar Allan Poe who wrote off the United States as a 'literary colony of Great Britain' was not the only writer to see it as a continent of intellectual poor relations – out of touch and behind the times.

London offered not only an escape from the tedium of American provincial life. Much more importantly, it gave aspiring authors the chance to publish what they had failed to publish in the United States. Herman Melville, for example, had to take his first novel *Typee* to London to find a buyer. At least if an author made a reputation in England, American critics were obliged to acknowledge it.

Henry James himself was well acquainted with Europe. His parents had travelled extensively there when he was a child. But it was London above all that

Tissot: Goodbye on the Mersey, Bridgeman Art Library

Leaving home
(left) Countless wealthy young Americans completed their education by making the 'Grand Tour' of Europe. Many more waved goodbye with no intention of returning. They accounted those they left behind bigoted, small-minded, unimaginative Philistines.

Quaint London Town
(right) Newcomers to London saw its streets, squares and homes with unjaundiced eyes. They tended to find what they were seeking: tradition, quaintness, solidity. Henry James did not look for Dickensian squalor, but gentility, style and good manners.

fascinated him: 'not a pleasant place; it is not agreeable, or cheerful or easy or exempt from reproach. It is only magnificent . . . on the whole the most possible form of life . . . the most complete compendium of the world.' He did, of course, choose to view the metropolis selectively – stripped of its Dickensian squalor – from the comfortable armchair of a gentleman's club.

There were several thriving colonies of artists and writers in London at that time, but the greatest concentration was in Chelsea. Among its American population, the network of Thameside streets harboured the writer Mark Twain, and the artists James McNeill Whistler and John Singer Sargent.

At 23 Tedworth Square, Mark Twain's avowed love of London survived bankruptcy, but was overshadowed by the death of his 24-year-old daughter Susy. On Sundays he walked by the canal in Regent's Park with his two surviving daughters in 'an atmosphere of world-loneliness'. On other days he would stroll down the King's Road among those he liked to call 'Shakespeare people'. Sometimes he would call on Henry James in Kensington. All the while, he wrote feverishly, until the grief passed.

PAINTERS AND POSERS

In London, American painters felt in easy reach of the new ideas germinating on the Continent. They also found a ready market for portrait paintings. Foremost among the portrait painters was John Singer Sargent. Although an American, he did not set eyes on the country until he was 20, and he was once described as 'an American born in Italy and educated in France, who dressed like a German, spoke like an Englishman, and painted like a Spaniard.'

After studying art in Paris, Sargent came to London and was taken by Henry James to art galleries, theatres and artists' studios. His style and ability to capture personality on canvas won him enormous popularity and success. Like James, he won the unqualified esteem of the English and was even offered the presidency of that archetypally British institution, the Royal Academy.

Every bit as widely travelled and cosmopolitan was the artist James McNeill Whistler who lived at various addresses in Chelsea's Tite Street and Cheyne Walk during his many years in England. Born in America, raised in Russia and educated in France, Whistler chose to live and paint in England. But he remained proud of his nationality, nostalgically reminding others that he was not only an American but a West Point man as well. He liked to invite British neighbours round for breakfast to impress on them the delights of all-American griddle cakes. Yet he gained a curious strength from his self-imposed exile, as it gave him a sense of his own value. Being an 'outsider', a rebel, was part of his unique artistic identity.

From his various houses near the Embankment, Whistler was in a good position to paint his famous nocturnal views of the Thames, or to row in the early hours of the morning. He and his faithful pupil Walter Greaves would also often row to Cremorne Gardens, a riverside amusement park with dancing, marionettes, beer gardens and bowling.

Whistler had little respect for his patrons, British or otherwise. Commissioned by the wealthy Liverpool

Mark Twain *(below) called London 'a collection of villages'. Lecturing to packed halls there, he gradually paid off his debts.*

25

Thameside Japan
The inspiration Whistler derived from the Thames did not confine him to painting London views. Variations in Flesh Colour and Green: The Balcony *(left), was inspired by Japanese prints but features a quite undisguised industrial Thames in the background.*

John Singer Sargent
(below), an expatriate American, became London's most popular portrait-painter – so much so that he sickened of the work and decided to 'abjure' the human face and 'paint nothing but Jehovah in Fulham Road'. His portraiture – the example on the right is of Mrs Charles Hunter – made him a rich celebrity. But when he was offered presidency of the Royal Academy he replied, 'I would do anything for the Royal Academy but that, and if you press me any more, I should flee the country.'

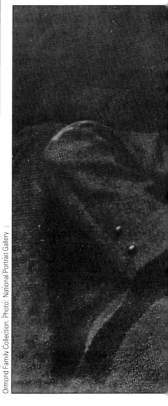

ship-owner Frederick Leyland to make minor aesthetic adjustments to one room in his newly refurbished house in Kensington, Whistler covered the prized leather wall-linings with pale blue paint and gold peacocks, ran up huge bills on his patron's account, then invited admirers to view his work. He even went so far as to tell Leyland to stay away, since *he* was of no interest to the visitors. 'He's only a millionaire,' said Whistler dismissively.

Although an expatriate, Whistler was a central figure in the British 'cult of Beauty' – the aesthetic movement. And down the road from him in Tite Street – at 'The House Beautiful' – lived perhaps the most famous exponent of aestheticism, Oscar Wilde. Wilde became the popular mouthpiece of the movement, and even went on a lecture tour in the United States to introduce Americans to the ideas of English aestheticism. But many of its theories originated from Whistler. The two

men – both renowned for their acerbic wit as much as for their flamboyant appearance – became friends, then rivals. At a fashionable lunchtime gathering at the Café Royal in Piccadilly (where writers and artists met to exchange ideas and gossip), Whistler made a particularly witty remark, at which Wilde commented 'I wish I had said that.' Whistler replied pointedly: 'You will, Oscar, you will.'

But Whistler's ready wit could not help him when he decided to take on the English art establishment and legal system. When the writer and critic John Ruskin accused him of 'flinging a pot of paint in the public's face' with his painting *Nocturne in Blue and Gold: The Falling Rocket*, Whistler's pride was hurt, and he sued. He won the case, but bankrupted himself in the process, and was finally obliged to exile himself in Venice.

Civilized and stimulating as London was, many of the American artistic set chose to escape, every so often,

Rixens: The Salon Lunch. Fine Art Photographic Library

Tate Gallery, London/Bridgeman Art Library

Cafés and restaurants
(right) were essential to the
artistic life. Shy poets of the
opposite sex met
unchaperoned over tea and
buns. The flamboyant
dandies of the Aesthetic
Movement held court,
during meals they could
rarely afford, and dazzled
followers with their wit.

Exiled to Venice
(below) Though Whistler
won his legal wrangle with
John Ruskin, the lawsuit
beggared him. As a result, he
was forced to sell up and live
in Venice for several years.

into the English countryside. They were in search of
the past, of a rural idyll, and found them in the quintes-
sentially English Cotswold village of Broadway. What
they created there probably bore little or no
resemblance to the rural life of any age, but a colony of
expatriates flourished.

The painter Francis Davis Millet, who arrived in
Broadway in 1884 with his family, liked nothing better
than to restore old buildings: he was an early conser-
vationist. Henry James and Edward Burne Jones (both

frequent visitors to Broadway) were of one mind in
believing that Millet and his wife had 'reconstructed the
Golden Age'.

Mary Anderson, a renowned American actress and
beauty, had come to the Cotswolds to escape nervous
exhaustion – and she stayed, despite all incentives
offered her to return to the United States. She made a
second 'beloved' centrepiece in this artistic community
which spent its time playing cricket and tennis and (according to the sunny recollections of one visitor) doing
'not much serious work . . . everything was food for
laughter'. Clearly the Broadway existence was a fairly
Bohemian one, for the painter Ned Abbey's puritanical
new wife found it impossible to live there. The couple
moved away to a purer rural idyll at Fairford in
Gloucestershire.

Perfect peace only suited the restless Americans for a
short while at a time. Most left Broadway in the winter,
although some, such as the writer Stephen Crane,

Federico del Campo: The Ca' d'Oro, Venice. Fine Art Photographic Library

27

Sources and Inspiration

Francis Millet: Between Two Fires. Tate Gallery, London

Eliot was to discover in himself an enormous sympathy for British behaviour, taste and humour, something which is reflected in his epic poem *The Wasteland*.

As he got older, Henry James found it increasingly pointless to differentiate between the English and the Americans. 'I can't look at the English-American world . . . save as a big Anglo-Saxon total, destined to such an amount of melting together.' After World War 1, there was never again to be such an intense cultural cross-fertilization between the two. But so complete was the assimilation of Americans into British cultural life between 1894 and 1914 that Virginia Woolf observed, 'Americans sink into us, over here, like raindrops into the sea'.

Antique England
(left) had passionate appeal for Americans. Francis Davis Millet set about 'recreating' it in the Cotswold village of Broadway, restoring old buildings and living out a rustic idyll. Realistic or not, it made a fertile artistic environment which attracted yet more American emigrés.

T.S. Eliot (1888-1965)
(below), a shy Harvard man, emigrated in 1915. But his 17th-century ancestors had lived in the rural peace of East Coker, Somerset. The Four Quartets retrace his family descent, to arrive at conclusions about time and God which were (and are) relevant to the American and English alike.

appear to have adopted the English countryside as a permanent home. Like most expatriates, Crane gravitated first to the circle of American writers in London. But he then bought Brede Manor near Rye where he enjoyed playing the English squire, writing his novels and entertaining house party guests in its great icy halls. It was probably Crane's lingering death at the age of 29 from tuberculosis, and the apparent indifference of his common-law wife Cora, that inspired James' novel *The Sacred Fount*.

The influx of Americans continued into the 20th century: 'Hardly a week goes by but I meet or hear of someone who goes into voluntary exile – some reporter who throws up a steady job to come to Europe and breathe; some professor from a freshwater college who comes away on scant savings. Our artists are all over Europe.' So wrote Ezra Pound when he joined that exodus in 1906, and travelled to England virtually penniless and knowing no-one. To him Europe represented a haven away from the mob – a refuge from too much democracy. 'The only way I could educate the educatable minority in the United States was to come to London . . . to the capital of the U.S. so far as art and letters and thought are concerned . . .'

Pound blustered his way into teaching at Regent Street Polytechnic and appointed himself the task of remaking English poetry. He established an informal agency in Kensington, and became a cantankerous literary impresario. His modest rooms soon saw a circle of writer friends, and he later wrote affectionately in his *Cantos* of those years and of 'our London, my London, your London'.

In 1913 a friend told Pound that 'there was a guy at Harvard doing funny stuff.' Before long the Harvard guy, T. S. Eliot, had come to England, and Pound was carving a place for him on the London artistic scene.

T. S. ELIOT

Caricature by Butterfield in Courier. Mary Evans Picture Library

28

H. G. WELLS

1866-1946

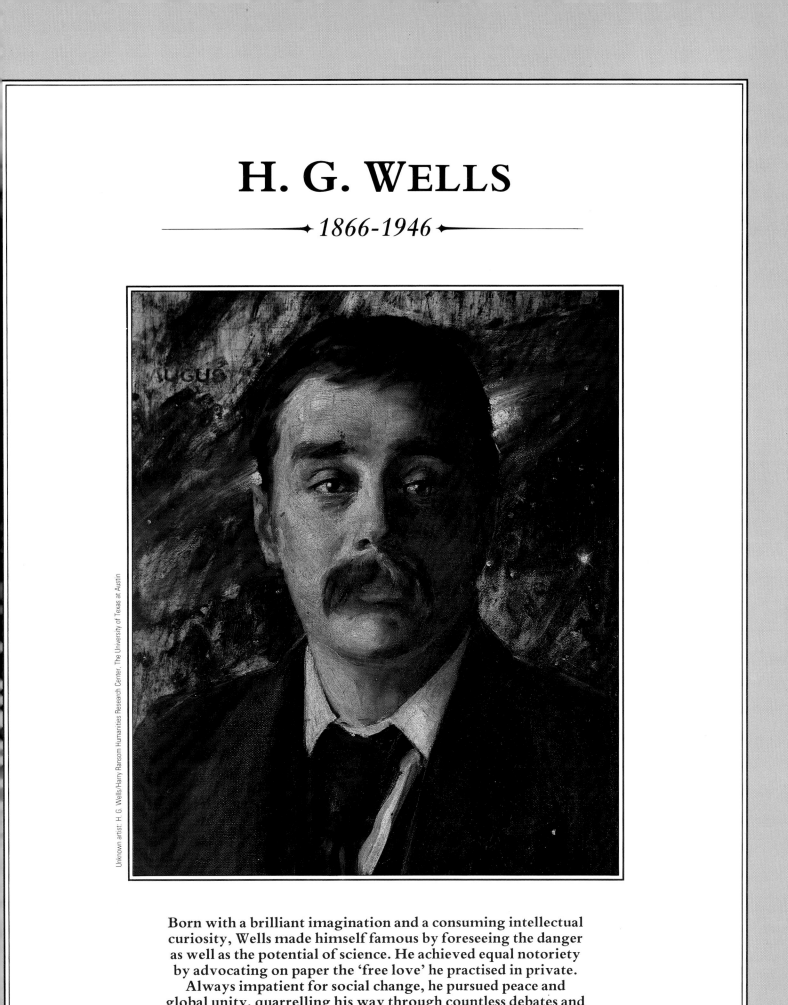

Born with a brilliant imagination and a consuming intellectual
curiosity, Wells made himself famous by foreseeing the danger
as well as the potential of science. He achieved equal notoriety
by advocating on paper the 'free love' he practised in private.
Always impatient for social change, he pursued peace and
global unity, quarrelling his way through countless debates and
articles, and often shifting ground. Vociferous and energetic in
pursuit of his beliefs, he was dubbed the 'great awakener of men'.

LUSTY AMBITIONS

Blessed with a powerful imagination and a thirst for knowledge, Wells escaped a life of insignificant drudgery and set himself forever at odds with the world of smug, repressive respectability.

One of H. G. Wells' most considerable and spectacular achievements is little known – his rise to fame from the humblest beginnings. He was born on 21 September in 1866 in Bromley, Kent, the youngest child of Sarah, a housemaid, and Joseph, a small-time shopkeeper. Wells' childhood betrayed no signs of the enormous success to come, and was probably most notable for loneliness. Sarah tried to stop him playing with other children because she had absorbed some of the snobbery of her employers and regarded his potential playmates as beneath him. To make matters worse, young Herbert George had little contact with his brothers because they were much older than him; while he was still at home, they were at school, and by the time he

A poor business
Joe and Sarah Wells (right) eked out 'a miserable half living' in a vermin-infested shop selling china and cricket gear. His lack of business sense and love of cricket so alienated her, that she began to impose her desire for social betterment on her gifted fourth child.

An avid student
H.G. makes an evolutionary joke of a skeleton (below) which the brilliant T. H. Huxley used for lectures.

Dr. M. J. Wells

ALFRED PARSONS.

Dr. M. J. Wells/Weidenfeld Archive

went to school, they had moved on.

Although Wells was an exceptionally bright pupil, he left school at 13 when his father's china shop went bankrupt. His lively, imaginative nature rebelled against the humdrum work he was offered over the next three years, both as a druggist's and as a draper's assistant, and he soon left both jobs. Another spell as a pupil-teacher ended almost as rapidly when the authorities discovered the headmaster had lied about his qualifications, and closed down the school.

NEW WORLDS

At about this time, Wells first discovered the wealth of books in the library and attic of the country house where his mother was then working. It sparked off his imagination, making him aware of the extraordinary worlds beyond the real one, waiting to be explored.

But despite this revelation, Wells had no career and was going nowhere until, at the age of 17, he tried to strike out by applying to his first headmaster for a teaching job. He was immediately hired

Key Dates

1866 born in Bromley, Kent

1879 apprentice draper

1891 marries cousin, Isabel Wells

1895 marries 'Jane' Robbins

1898 *The War of the Worlds*

1909 'elopes' with Amber Reeves

1912 meets Rebecca West

1914 birth of their son, Anthony

1934 interviews Stalin and Roosevelt

1946 dies in London

Apprentice draper
'Almost as unquestioning as her belief in Our Father and Our Saviour was her belief in drapers', said H.G. of his mother. When money ran out, she took H.G. (now aged 14) away from school, and apprenticed him at a draper's (below) opposite the gates of Windsor Castle (left).

continued his writing. Then in 1890 he fell in love with his beautiful young cousin, Isabel Mary Wells, and married her the following June.

The marriage soon disintegrated, however. The two seemed emotionally, sexually, and intellectually incompatible, and Wells, never monogamous by temperament, embarked on a series of affairs. Of these, the most emotionally rewarding was his relationship with one of his students, Amy Catherine 'Jane' Robbins.

It was during the course of this affair that Wells fell ill. He began coughing up blood and went to recuperate from a minor haemorrhage in Eastbourne. Here he dashed off an article for a newspaper and was amazed that not only was it accepted, but they wanted more of the same.

LIBERATION AT LAST

This sudden, minor, literary success did wonders for Wells. He decided to abandon his relationship with Mary for a life with Jane, and this liberation led to an outpouring of brilliant articles and short stories. From 1895, when he married Jane, to 1898, he wrote four of his most popular novels, *The Time Machine, The Island of Dr Moreau, The Invisible Man* and *The War of the Worlds.*

Wells' theory that science afforded infinite possibilities for creating a better world and his daring handling of the new genre of science fiction became instant hits. The critics raved and publishers tripled their advances. But Wells still had one major problem. He had never been healthy (even the earliest descriptions of him depict a timid, weak boy), and had recently suffered a second haemorrhage. In addition he was supporting both his current wife and his ex-wife, and when he decided in 1899 to visit Mary for the first time in five years, the emotional strain proved too much for him. He suffered what could be termed a breakdown and became morbidly aware of his

and thrived in academe, studying science in his spare time. He won a scholarship to the Normal School of Science (now Imperial College) in London, where he was taught by some of the finest minds of his time, notably the biologist Thomas Huxley. Huxley, like Charles Darwin, was one of the leaders of a scientific revolution propelling people out of the Victorian age at a far quicker pace than many could tolerate. Wells, however, devoured Huxley's theories on the origins and purpose of life, although he rapidly lost interest in his studies when allocated less inspiring teachers.

He left college without a degree, but took it externally in 1890, gaining first-class honours in zoology. He had by now acquired three life-long passions: women, social reform and writing. When Wells was 21, he made for London to write his great novel. But when it was finished he was so dissatisfied with his 35,000-word 'magnum opus' that he threw it into the fire. It seemed that he would never rise above a teaching career with its demoralizingly low income, and he spent the next three years in the classroom, although he still

'Very innocent lovers'
'I was always wanting to board and storm and subjugate her imagination so that it would come out . . . to meet mine', wrote Wells of his first wife, Isabel (right) – but, 'it never came out to meet me.' Nor, apparently, did she delight in sex. Wells quickly felt trapped by this marriage and found the only answer was to replace 'simple honesty . . . by duplicity'. He took lovers. 'I wanted to compensate myself for the humiliation she had so unwittingly put upon me.'

Second marriage
Wells left Isabel for his pupil, 'Jane' Robbins (above). Sexually, Jane was as 'innocent and ignorant' as Isabel, but she was sympathetic to his work and his ideas on personal freedom.

Wells' friendship with other important writers including Joseph Conrad, Ford Madox Ford, George Gissing, and even Henry James.

Wells' second marriage, however, was by now faring badly. After the birth of two sons, George and Frank, in 1901 and 1903 respectively, Wells lost interest in Jane. They agreed to cease being lovers and, with Jane's consent, Wells looked elsewhere for intellectual and sexual excitement.

A DIFFICULT ROLE

Jane was well aware that there was a hollow core to their marriage, but was nonetheless determined to remain his wife. As she saw it, she still had a crucial role to play in his life, raising their children, keeping the family home for when he chose to return to it and organizing his work. She became an indispensable anchor, and in return enjoyed being the wife of one of the greatest writers of the time. It was a lonely, difficult role, but gradually Jane developed her own life and her own group of friends.

Meanwhile, Wells' interest in sex was extending beyond the physical. Sex, along with religion and science, were the three elements of his furious attack on current morality. He wanted to sweep away the Victorian ethics which he thought were strangling the modern world. Sex should now be

mortality. Yet it was precisely this likelihood of an early death that drove him to write more and better novels.

Another beneficial effect of this setback was that the Royal Literary Fund, worried about his finances, asked several prominent writers to approach him on their behalf to discover whether he needed a loan. Fortunately Wells' books were selling too well for that, but the offer did lead to

The public image
Given Wells' astonishing beliefs and scandalous lifestyle, the public both laughed and marvelled at him. Punch pictured him on a flying machine (above). Max Beerbohm drew a cartoon of the older Wells debating with his younger self (left) – indicating how greatly his opinions changed over the years.

REBECCA WEST

Although Wells had two wives and count-less amours, his most important lover was Rebecca West. Her real name was Cicily Fairfield: at 19 she adopted 'Rebecca', after a fictional heroine. The same year, she met Wells, a man of 46, at the height of his fame. Her own gifts were not immediately apparent to him, but when, in a review of his book *The Passionate Friends,* she endorsed his views on casual sex, he decided an affair might thrive.

They called each other by pet names, she Panther, he Jaguar, denoting their fierce, anti-social mutuality. A son, Anthony, was born in 1914, and Rebecca lived by writing fem-inist articles, witty, hard-hitting reviews and novels. It was she who finally ended the affair. At 38 she married another man, and went on to produce a mammoth study of Yugoslavia, report the Nuremberg Trials (of war-criminals) and write numerous articles on topical spy scandals. She was made a Dame for her ser-vices to literature, and was still writing within months of her death in 1983.

Cocking a snook
(below) A rare secular stained-glass window illustrates the Fabian Society at the time Wells took issue with it. He is seen in the bottom corner, thumbing his nose at the other members. Wells believed in sweeping away the old order, rather than using established channels for political change. He was therefore perpetually at odds with his fellow Fabians – but they always forgave him. George Bernard Shaw wrote that, 'unhindered, unpunished, apparently even undisliked . . . the worse he behaved the more he was indulged, and the more he was indulged the worse he behaved.'

freely discussed and experienced because his vision of a better society was dependent on people leading fulfilled lives, sexually and intellectually. But while the public were excited by Wells' bold descriptions of a new world in which he had welded a poetic vision on to scientific possibilities, few were ready for sexual liberation.

Wells' passionate desire to steer humanity to a better world led to further problems when, in his mid-30s, he joined the Fabian Society. The Fabians also wanted to restructure society, but worked for an intellectual, not a violent revolution. This was much too frustrating for the ever impatient Wells, and in one of the great debates of the time he was challenged by the brilliant Irish playwright George Bernard Shaw to thrash out Fabian policy. Few people could defeat the prodigiously witty and intellectually agile Shaw, let alone Wells, who was not a particularly good speaker or debater. Shaw proclaimed him to be a dreamer of hollow visions who was incapable of working out the complexities of a utopia. Soundly beaten, Wells left the Fabians one year later to found his 'New Republic' through other means. It may be, however, that his decision to quit was also prompted by the fact that he had recently seduced the daughters of two fellow members, one of whom, Amber Reeves, was now pregnant.

Wells ran away with Amber to France, but finding her unequal to the task of looking after him, reverted periodically to Jane, soon suggesting that Amber find herself a husband. Reluctantly she agreed, but Wells continued their affair after her marriage and the birth of his child.

This gave him the material for the novel *Ann Veronica,* in which a liberated young girl rejects convention to become a suffragette, and even-tually runs off with an older man. In it Wells refuted the concept of honour, maintaining that not only should a woman yield to any strong sexual temptations, but that she should be proud of having done so. His editors at Macmillans thought it too scandalous to publish, and when it did appear the right-wing critics tore it apart. The fuss died down with his next immensely successful novel, *Mr Polly,* but flared up again with the contentious *New Machiavelli.* Libraries banned the book and Wells left for France to rethink his position, outraged that the world was ignoring his rallying cry.

A MEETING OF MINDS

One person who did understand him, however, was the future novelist Rebecca West. They met in 1912 when Wells, aged 46, was at the height of his fame, and Rebecca West was a radical, attractive 19-year-old. She had written a scathing review of one of his books – which intrigued him – and, after resolving apparent differences, they became lovers. Their affair spanned the next ten years and produced a son, Anthony West, born in 1914. The first four years were among the happiest, most exciting in Wells' life. World War I was looming and to Wells it spelt the promise of a new world – the dead values of the past would be blown away leaving Wells, the self-appointed prophet, to guide his people to the Promised Land.

But before the war had ended, both public and private worlds were collapsing. Rebecca West began to have grave misgivings about sacrificing her career and life to Wells, who was becoming increasingly self-centred and unreliable. And 'The War That Will End War', as Wells had called it, had turned into a mindless slaughter.

On a personal level this was a remarkably hectic time for Wells: he was living at three separate addresses (his private London flat, in Essex with Jane, and wherever Rebecca happened to be); he had had a huge success with *Mr Britling Sees it Through* (reprinted 12 times in the last three months of 1916); and early in 1918 he joined the Department of Propaganda based at Whitehall.

'I AM REALLY FAMOUS'

Because Wells' principal interest was fighting for a new world state which would end wars between individual countries, he soon resigned from his post of Propaganda adviser. To help the world's leading statesmen to realize this aim, as Europe emerged from the end of the war, he researched his massive *Outline of History* to help them better understand their task. Ironically, the very people for whom he had been writing ignored it, and academics scoffed at its eccentricities, gaps and inaccuracies. But Wells' readers loved it, buying over 100,000 copies.

Meanwhile Wells was invited to the United States; his fame preceded him, much to his astonishment and delight. The papers reported everything he did and said, so that Wells had to acknowledge, 'I am really famous here, people turn round in the street and when I went to a play the house stood up and clapped.' He was rapidly turning into an international star and in 1920

went on a visit to Russia where he discussed the future of the world – and particularly of Russia – with the revolutionary Lenin.

From 1920, however, it gradually became clear that Wells was not going to get it all his own way, in private or public. Although Rebecca West regarded him as 'everything one imagines in a genius', she eventually realized that the affair was blotting out her own rich prospects. Wells could neither leave Jane nor marry Rebecca and so, in 1923, as Rebecca later wrote, 'we parted like lovers . . . and you exploded into rage and hate in the afternoon.' Rebecca kept Anthony and Wells agreed to support him.

More trouble followed when Wells reacted to this rejection by throwing himself into an affair with a 30-year old Austrian translator. When he then suddenly abandoned her, she tried to commit suicide in his flat. Any hopes he had of hiding this, or the sham of his marriage to Jane, were ruined when the newspapers headlined the story the following day.

Wells' political life fared little better. It was now certain that despite his immense popularity and meetings with the top politicians of the day his grand design for a new world had come to nothing. He regarded himself as 'a man lit by a vision of the world . . . yet powerless to realise it.' Despite these setbacks, Wells rarely slipped into self-pity, but worked relentlessly for his new world, and still published novels.

In 1927 came another major blow. Wells had been spending an increasing amount of time in France because of ill health, and in June that year

Under fire
As the Blitz (above) raged round his London flat, Wells continued to write. The War gave proof of his darkest visions of scientific 'progress' leading to human destruction.

Meeting with a leader
In 1920 Wells interviewed Lenin (left) for the Sunday Express. *Though Wells had cheered on the 1917 Revolution and considered Lenin 'a very great man', he was sceptical of Lenin's economic plans for Russia. 'Come back and see us in ten years' time', was Lenin's retort. Wells' Express articles were sympathetic to the Bolshevik state, and he remained an important interpreter of Russia to the West.*

Novosti

Fact or Fiction

THE GREAT HOAX

In 1938 Orson Welles made an American radio adaptation of *The War of the Worlds* for transmission on Hallowe'en. Those tuning in late, unwarned, heard fake newscasts followed by 'President Roosevelt' exhorting the nation to remain calm and an 'eye-witness account' of the destruction of New York. All over the country, thousands panicked and fled their homes. Although he denied it, Orson Welles was secretly delighted by the success of his ruse.

---

misuse of science – proved all too well founded when the United States dropped two atom bombs on Japan.

By now, Wells was desperately ill, although his mind still forced his ailing body to write. But by midsummer 1946, he was too ill to go on. The man who had enjoyed the affections of so many women died alone in his flat on 13 August.

Wells had risen from a frail, reticent, shabbily dressed shop boy to become the prophet of his generation, and at his funeral, writers, politicians and statesmen assembled together. As Clement Atlee said, the world from now on will seem silent without 'The great awakener of men'.

Renewed fame

Wells' novels won a second lease of life and his celebrity status soared as soon as film techniques were able to do justice to his epic visions. Pictured below arriving at the London premiere of The Shape of Things to Come, *Wells revelled in the fame and adulation.*

was accompanied by Jane when invited to a lecture at the Sorbonne in Paris. Not long after, Jane was diagnosed as having cancer. She died later that year leaving Wells distraught by her loss. In addition, he had to face up to the possibility that his illegitimate son Anthony might also die. Six months later, in 1928, Anthony went down with tuberculosis at the same time that Rebecca became ill with influenza. These catastrophes, as Wells wrote to her, reopen 'all sorts of shut-down tendernesses and I feel like your dear brother and your best friend and your father and your once (and not quite forgetting it) lover.'

But these links with the past were soon ended. Rebecca married in 1930, the same year that Wells sold his old house where he had lived with Jane. Thereafter, until his death, he lived close to Regent's Park in London. Although no longer in the best-selling lists, Wells was by no means forgotten. In 1934 he tackled the world's two most powerful leaders, having interviews with Stalin in Russia and Theodore Roosevelt in America, in order to find common ground that could be the basis of future civilization.

The outbreak of World War II signified the collapse of the core of his life's work. Plans for a peaceful world state were daily blasted as bombs exploded around his flat in central London. And finally, in 1945, one of his earliest fears – the

THE WAR OF THE WORLDS

An intriguing other-world curiosity gradually takes on the dread dimensions of catastrophe, as Wells' narrator struggles to survive "the rout of civilisation . . . the massacre of mankind".

Written at a time when British society was still marvelling at the bicycle, *The War of the Worlds* is a Victorian novel that foresees such 20th-century phenomena as chemical warfare, laser beams, the dominance of man by machine, and, most ominously, war on a scale that could annihilate the whole of civilization. Wells described his previous novels, *The Time Machine* and *The Island of Dr Moreau,* as 'science romances', but *The War of the Worlds* is better described as science-horror. It is one of the first treatments of what subsequently became a science-fiction cliché – the arrival on our planet of the Thing from Outer Space. The novel's additional power draws on the traditions of the horror story in which 'normality' is threatened by the paranormal.

The idea for the story was furnished by the author's brother, Frank. 'How would it be, ' he said to Wells one night, 'if some creatures of vastly superior power suddenly came down upon us and behaved like a drunken man-of-war's crew let loose amongst some gentle savages?' During a walk two days later on Horsell Common, Woking – where the Martians first land in the story – Wells began to visualize the action.

GUIDE TO THE PLOT

Narrated in flashback by a writer-philosopher six years after the event, the story begins when a mysterious cylindrical object lands on the Common. When it unscrews, a creature appears who fills the narrator with disgust and dread: "Then something resembling a little grey snake, about the thickness of a walking stick, coiled up out of the writing middle and wriggled in the air towards me."

When a human deputation approaches

Unleashed terror
As the Martians emerge from the pit, the narrator drives his wife (left) to a 'safe' distance. Behind him, the invaders are "setting fire to everything within range of their Heat-Ray".

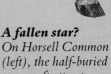

A fallen star?
On Horsell Common (left), the half-buried spacecraft attracts some curious on-lookers, including the narrator – to whom the latest technology represents nothing more advanced than his bicycle.

Exodus from London
(right) The city was in flight: "people were being trampled and crushed . . . revolvers were fired, people stabbed, and the policemen . . . were breaking the heads of the people they were called out to protect."

this creature, there is a flash of light, and an "invisible, inevitable sword of heat" kills everyone in its path. Horrified, the narrator flees the scene.

For a few hours, he can hardly come to terms with what he has seen, and life slips into its routine pattern. However, when he returns to the scene (fired with "something of my old schoolboy dreams of heroism and battle") fighting begins between the newly arrived army and the aliens. It soon becomes apparent that the soldiers are no match for the invaders. A "poisoned dart" seems to have been stuck into planet Earth, and the "commonplace habits of our social order" buckle under the pressure of events which ultimately "topple that social order headlong".

Having ensured his wife's safety by taking her to stay with his cousin in Leatherhead, the narrator returns to the fray, his fear overcome by his consuming fascination with what is happening. He sees more evidence of Martian destruction and of the arrival of another cylinder. He also manages to get a close view of the aliens' Fighting Machine, which he describes as "a monstrous tripod . . . a walking engine of glittering metal". The Martians' murderous efficiency is graphically con-

> *"It came to me that I was upon this dark common, helpless, unprotected and alone. Suddenly like a thing falling upon me from without came – Fear. . . . I ran weeping silently as a child might do. Once I had turned, I did not dare to look back."*

"They wiped us out"
The Artillery (above) are no match for the monstrous technology of the Martians, as a solitary survivor witnesses.

veyed by an artilleryman who tells him that "they wiped us out – simply wiped us out". In a telling phrase that seems to anticipate not only the coming century's world wars, but also the possibility of complete global destruction, the narrator comments: "Never before in the history of warfare has destruction been so indiscriminate and so universal."

From here, the novel charts an exciting, terrifying escalation of disaster, as the Martians relentlessly continue on their path of destruction. The shifting colours –

black, red, green – of atmosphere, sky and trees, are evidence of the poisonous vapours emitted by the Martians, and signify the infection of human society by the invasion. The perspective of the tale widens to encompass London and the experiences of the narrator's younger brother. In his flight from the capital, he assists two ladies in a pony chaise who are being attacked by desperate thugs. Fear leads to frenzied attempts at self-preservation. Engulfed by a tidal wave of panic, the civilized cities of England are becoming living hells of horror and pain.

Meanwhile, the narrator has fallen in with a curate, who is mentally devastated by the invasion. They are in the narrator's home when another of the Martians' cylinders hits the house and buries them under the ruins. In the days of hunger, tension and claustrophobia that follow, the curate becomes steadily more danger-ous and deranged, and eventually the narrator has to kill him to prevent him revealing their whereabouts to the aliens. When the narrator finally emerges from the ruins, he steps into a completely changed world: "For a time I believed that mankind had been swept out of existence and that I stood there alone, the last man left alive."

Because of the novel's flashback tech-nique, we know that the narrator will

survive. Yet there are still two surprising revelations to come: another encounter with the artilleryman, whose personality has been completely warped by his experience; and the deliberately anti-climactic defeat of the Martians which comes from a wholly unexpected source.

A FANTASY-THRILLER

Wells' story is a thriller packed with ideas. Although a fantasy, it has a realistic base that gives it conviction: Wells is equally precise about the imaginative detail of how the Martians function, as he is about the topographical detail of the English countryside which they are systemati cally laying waste. The author conveys the mass hysteria of the population with a cinematographic aerial shot:

"... If one could have hung that morning in a balloon in the blazing blue above London, every northward and eastward road running out of the infinite tangle of streets would have seemed stippled black with the streaming fugitives, each dot a human agony of terror and physical distress."

Yet the real merits of the novel lie less in its description or drama than in its ideas. The main theme is Wells' attack on human arrogance.

At the beginning of the novel, when the narrator explains the reason for the Mar-tian invasion (their planet has cooled to

Peter Mennin

"Giants in armour"
(left) The formless mass of the Martian body contrasts with the agile, metal Fighting Machines they build for themselves. Some scoff at these "boilers on legs", but not for long. As boats full of refugees crowd the Thames Estuary, only the ironclad warship Thunder Child *stands between them and destruction by the Martians.*

Deadly tentacle
(below) In his lust to survive, the narrator brutally silences the raving curate, then must watch a "long, metallic snake of tentacle" grope its way towards the smell of blood.

the point where their survival is threatened unless they adopt a warmer habitat), he makes a comparison between their violent action and "the ruthless and utter destruction our own species has wrought, not only upon animals, such as the vanished bison and dodo, but on its own inferior races."

The effect of the Martian invasion is to reduce man from master to slave, from colonizer to colonized. The lesson learnt could be salutary if it teaches us "pity – pity for those witless souls that suffer our domination." In this sense, Wells' novel belongs unexpectedly with other contemporary stories such as Kipling's *The Man Who Would be King* and Conrad's *Heart of Darkness* – grotesque and ironic parables about British Imperialism.

> *"Why are these things permitted? What sins have we done? ...fire, earthquake, death! As if it were Sodom and Gomorrah! All our work undone, all the work...What are these Martians?"*
>
> *"What are we?"* I answered.

"With infinite complacency", says the narrator at the beginning, "men went to and fro over this globe about their little affairs, secure in their assurance of their empire over matter." Part of Wells' strategy in the novel is to demolish such assurance and complacency. Because it is outside their experience, the civilians are shown to be remarkably slow in appreciating the menace of the Martians.

When full realization dawns, the human reaction is not one of united resistance but of selfish desperation. How fragile civilization must be, says Wells, if it can disintegrate so quickly under pressure. Conventional and chivalric values collapse, and the narrator himself is implicated in this, in his rage and exasperation against the curate.

Wells has contrived a calamitous situation that is completely outside human control: it is neither caused by human agency nor ended by it. This situation questions the Victorians' unthinking trust in the idea of progress. "In the larger design of the universe", concludes the narrator, "this invasion from Mars is not without its ultimate benefit for men: it has robbed us

of that serene confidence in the future which is the most fruitful source of decadence . . . " The Martians themselves could be a warning about the next stage of man's development: a higher intelligence and a greater technological sophistication, but at the expense of artistic sensibility and human sympathy. Looking at our present century, who could say that Wells' apprehensions have proved unfounded?

The War of the Worlds keeps all its appeal, even with the passage of time. Small wonder it has inspired films and dramatizations, although in the 1953 film version the emphasis of the story was altered to a narrower theme: the Martian invasion of Earth is equated with Marxist infiltration of America. In its time, it forced people to think about the unthinkable – about having to survive in a depopulated, demoralized, devastated universe. In our own time, the unthinkable has crept ever nearer, and a work written in 1898 seems no less relevant as we approach the year 2001. Nearly 50 years after his death, H. G. Wells is still entitled to the biting epitaph he penned for himself:

'I told you so – you *damned* fools.'

In the Background

THE BATTLE OF DORKING

Sir George Chesney, in his 1871 novel (below), imagined a German army invading a badly armed, ill-prepared England. He achieved realism by setting the action in quiet Surrey countryside. Wells used the same idea (and setting) for his Martian invasion.

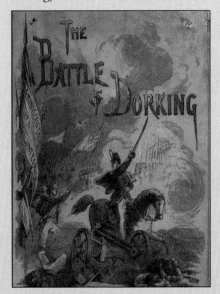

CHARACTERS IN FOCUS

E.M. Forster claimed that Wells' characters were 'as flat as a photograph'. *The War of the Worlds* bears this out: Wells is more interested in the excitement of a situation or an idea than in characterization. He presents, rather, a range of typical emotional responses to calamity, from capable to cowardly, fearless to fascist. Even so, the four main characters, if not psychologically complex, spring vividly to life.

WHO'S WHO

The narrator A progressive thinker, who, after the invasion, becomes "a battleground of fear and curiosity".

The narrator's brother A medical student based in London, who – usefully – proves himself to be "an expert boxer".

The curate A distraught, destroyed man who encounters the narrator during the Martian advance and is trapped with him in a ruined house.

The artillery-man An ordinary soldier, who later arms himself with a cutlass. His ideas become as wild as his transformed appearance.

Ogilvy A scientific friend of the narrator, and one of the first to notice the intermittent flashes on the surface of distant Mars.

Stent The Astronomer Royal, who joins Ogilvy and others on Horsell Common to study the aliens. They all meet the same fate.

Mrs Elphinstone A woman who is rescued by the narrator's brother, after traditional notions of decency and chivalry have given way to violence and desperate attempts at self-preservation.

The narrator's wife A symbol of helpless, vulnerable tenderness, she represents to the narrator everything harmonious and pleasant which will be destroyed by the time the Martians have completed their rout.

The artilleryman, "in a perfect passion of emotion" (above), takes refuge in the narrator's house after his battery is wiped out by Martians. Though he recovers his self-control, he reaches despairing conclusions: "We're down; we're beat", and finds a perverse joy in thinking of all the petty taboos that will be swept away, like "eating peas with a knife".

The Martian (above), whether repulsively naked, with its "fungoid . . . oily brown skin", or armoured in its Handling or Fighting Machine, has an intellect "vast and cool and unsympathetic", which looks on humans as mere "eatable ants". At first it seems that gravity will keep the invaders grounded in their pit, but nobody allows for the technical genius of these implacable killers.

The narrator (left) is a writer, philosopher and scientist. Because of his cast of mind, he cannot help but investigate and speculate on the Martians' progress. We are invited to share both his terror and his curiosity. On his own admission, his failings include cowardly panic and uncontrollable violence – as the curate finds to his cost. But he is not essentially a man of action, for this is a novel intended to make us think, rather than merely to excite.

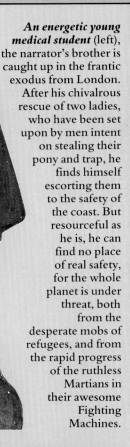

An energetic young medical student (left), the narrator's brother is caught up in the frantic exodus from London. After his chivalrous rescue of two ladies, who have been set upon by men intent on stealing their pony and trap, he finds himself escorting them to the safety of the coast. But resourceful as he is, he can find no place of real safety, for the whole planet is under threat, both from the desperate mobs of refugees, and from the rapid progress of the ruthless Martians in their awesome Fighting Machines.

The fragile memory of his wife (right) is central to the narrator's sense of what the Martians have destroyed – "the old life of hope and tender helpfulness ceased for ever". His attempt to protect her is fruitless, as the place of retreat to which he takes her is razed to the ground.

The curate (left) betrays "a fair weakness" in his face that indicates his character. Strolling one morning down a country lane, composing his sermon, his world is turned upside down as marauding Martians slaughter the populace. His faith, under trial, provides no answers to this wholesale destruction, and without his faith the curate descends into madness and invites the narrator's contempt.

TIME-TRAVELLER

Drawing on past and present, on scientific fact and personal experience, Wells sought to predict and warn of the shape of things to come.

It was once proposed by H. G. Wells that every university should appoint a professor of the future. His suggestion was never taken up, but Wells himself could be described as the world's first unofficial futurologist. Predicting or attempting to shape the future is the most important single theme in his incredibly prolific output – over 40 novels, a great many stories, dozens of books of reportage, reflections, projections and plans, a 200,000-word *Essay in Autobiography* (1934) and a supplementary volume on his sexual adventures.

Fellow-writer Joseph Conrad dedicated his novel *The Secret Agent* to Wells as 'The Historian of the Ages to Come', and another friend and fellow-novelist, Frank Swinnerton, noted that 'H. G.' was 'the first scientific novelist in English literature' as well as 'the champion surprise packet of the literary world'.

Wells made his reputation in the 1890s with a series of scientific romances includ-

Invisible Man, of scientific discovery being harnessed for evil purposes; and the shattering vision at the end of *The Island of Dr Moreau* (1896), of ordinary men and women as "animals half-wrought into the outward image of human souls" who "would presently begin to revert, to show first this bestial mark and then that". Within a few more years, however, Wells was recognized as a futurologist on a more mundane plane, as reality caught up with his description of 'land ironclads' – tanks – in a short story, and the scenes of devastation in *The War in the Air* (1908) became increasingly plausible.

NOVELIST, PROPHET AND PLANNER

In the 1900s Wells wrote fewer scientific romances (the last was *The World Set Free*, 1914) and embarked on his extraordinary double career as a novelist and prophet/planner of a new social order. *Anticipations* (1901) and *A Modern Utopia* (1905) contain

Wells' earliest blueprints for the scientifically organized, peaceful, co-operative world of social and sexual equality which he never ceased to work for. A fictional counterpart, *In the Days of the Comet* (1906), pictured the society created by a human race mysteriously made sane and reasonable by the passage

Long-suffering wife
Jane Wells, the author's second wife, typed all his manuscripts as well as looking after their two sons and running his house. She remained constant to him in spite of his many affairs, and he continued to rely heavily on her for practical and moral support, seeking and valuing her opinion on all his writings.

ing *The Time Machine* (1895), *The War of the Worlds* (1898) and *The Invisible Man* (1897), works that established such durable science fiction categories as time travel and invasion by aliens (often 'bug-eyed monsters'). Readers and critics, dazzled by Wells' skilful mixture of science and fantasy, hardly noticed the wider implications in his writing – the consequence of class exploitation in *The Time Machine;* the possibility, raised in *The*

Amazing success
The mixture of imagination with scientific possibilities proved a potent formula for Wells.

Dr. M. J. Wells/Weidenfeld Archive

of a comet; since the results included sexual liberty, the book caused a considerable scandal.

Most of Wells' novels during this period touched on social problems more obliquely, often incorporating large slices of autobiography. Wells defended this practice on the grounds that 'It is only by giving from his own life and feeling that a writer gives life to a character. Writers are like God in this at least, that they make men in their own image and their own breath gives them such life as they have.'

Love and Mr Lewisham (1900), *Ann Veronica* (1909) and *The New Machiavelli* (1910) draw liberally on Wells' teaching career, his marriages and sexual adventures, and his involvement with Fabian socialism and feminism; the references to real people and situations were obvious enough to compound the scandal created by his advocacy of 'free love' in *In the Days of the Comet*.

SWITCHING TO SATIRE

Astonishingly, Wells emerged as a major comic novelist during the very years when he was simultaneously functioning as scientific romancer, social prophet and 'serious' novelist. In *Kipps* (1905) and *The History of Mr Polly* (1910) he created vital, idiosyncratic characters that have often been compared admiringly with those of Charles Dickens. Artie Kipps and Alfred Polly are 'little men', sprung from the same undernourished, ill-educated shop-worker class as Wells himself, and generations of readers have enjoyed their verbal blunders and misadventures. But there is

Hidden treasures
The library at Uppark (above), where Wells' mother was a housemaid, provided the boy with his first taste of literature. But a far greater discovery were the works of more radical writers, stacked away in an attic room.

also pointed social satire in their stories, and a characteristic moral in the case of Mr Polly, who discovers that "If you don't like your life you can change it."

Rich comedy underlies *Tono-Bungay* (1909), but this novel is built on a much larger scale, painting a damning picture of the hypocrisy of Edwardian society. Many readers have agreed with the author, who was 'disposed to regard it as the finest and most finished novel upon accepted lines' that he had written.

Wells was deeply shaken by the 1914–18

Self-portrait
Here Wells shows himself, like his hero Mr Lewisham, busily writing.

For and against
Shaw (below left) often supported Wells' ideas, while Belloc and Chesterton (right) raged against them.

Mansell Collection

Korda Films/Central Independent Television

W·M·301.

War, which for him represented an utter collapse of progressive civilization. In response, he redoubled his efforts to set humankind on a saner path, and much of his later fiction constitutes a thinly disguised excuse for the urgent discussion of his ideas. Although still capable of writing a gripping 'history of the future' (*The Shape of Things to Come*, 1933), his chief ambition was to be an educator.

With *The Outline of History* (1920) Wells aimed to replace the narrow nationalistic teaching of contemporary schools with a wider vision of 'the common story of mankind', viewed as an exciting collective endeavour. There had been nothing like it before. Wells' *Outline* was first issued in 24 fortnightly parts, and reached a huge public; during Wells' lifetime the book sold at least a million copies. Having performed a similar service for biology and social studies with *The Science of Life* (1930) and *The Work, Wealth and Happiness of Mankind* (1931), Wells was recognized as 'the greatest international scientific educator of his time'.

The effort was imperative, since 'Human history becomes more and more a race between education and catastrophe'. Though often portrayed as a simple-minded believer in the inevitability of progress, Wells in fact had a strong pessimistic streak. The scientific romances are hardly reassuring in their vision of human destiny, and in his other work Wells often stated that human

Triumph of technology
The film version of The Shape of Things to Come, *with its extraordinary sets and powerful vision of the future, stunned cinema audiences in 1936.*

Fame and notoriety
To his surprise, Wells found his Short History of the World *a fantastic money-spinner, although his view of history caused offence to some.*

survival was possible rather than likely. Even in his last writings he alternated between a qualified optimism and outright despair. He hoped that 'the human mind may be in a phase of transition to a new, fearless, clear-headed way of living', but in another mood predicted that Man was finished – that 'The stars in their courses have turned against him and he has to give place to some other animal'.

FULL OF IDEAS

As a novelist, Wells had something of the fertility and casualness of the great Victorian writers; he confessed that 'the larger part of my fiction was written lightly and with a certain haste'. The Wellsian novel, high-spirited, loosely structured and brimming over with ideas, did not altogether please more artistically conscious writers such as Henry James. He and Wells finally quarrelled when the venerable master craftsman declared himself unable to take Wells' work seriously, nor to account it literature. It seems that James wanted to teach Wells his craft and Wells, having published 30 successful novels, strongly resented his patronizing stance. But although Wells sometimes declared himself a journalist rather than an artist, he in fact had his own vision of literature as 'the thought and expressed intention of the race', and of the novelist as 'the most potent of artists'. 'Before we have done', he predicted, 'we will have all life within the scope of the novel' – a forecast of the future that Wells himself fulfilled.

BBC Hulton Picture Library

Extraordinarily prolific and talented, H. G. Wells enjoyed several different reputations during his long literary career. He pioneered fundamental themes of science fiction, including time travel (*The Time Machine*, 1895) and aliens from outer space (*The War of the Worlds*, 1898). He met with such success that his contemporaries hardly noticed the wider and more sinister implications of the master-vivisectionist in *The Island of Dr Moreau* (1896), or of the abuse of scientific knowledge in *The Invisible Man* (1897).

Later Wells emerged as the comic bard of the disadvantaged 'little man' in *Kipps* (1905) and *The History of Mr Polly* (1910). Almost simultaneously he was publishing 'serious' novels, including *Tono-Bungay* (1909), focusing on the less agreeable side of Edwardian society, and the controversial *Ann Veronica* (1909). Wells followed these works with many novels of ideas, educational pieces and projects of social and political reform, remaining for decades one of the major intellectual forces of his time.

THE TIME MACHINE

+ 1895 +

Surrounded by the Eloi (below), a beautiful yet strangely impassive people, the hero of this short novel is a Victorian Englishman known only as the Time Traveller. Finding himself in the year AD 802 701, his time machine is stolen and in searching for it he penetrates into a dim underground world where giant engines throb. There he discovers another people, repulsive creatures of darkness known as the Morlocks, who prey on the Eloi. After many adventures the Morlocks capture Weena, an Eloi girl whose life the Time Traveller has saved. So much he tells his incredulous friends on his return to his own time. Then he sets off again – to rescue Weena perhaps . . .

THE ISLAND OF DR MOREAU

+ 1896 +

A pack of wild, misshapen creatures (above) descend on and terrify a shipwrecked visitor, Edward Prendick. The other inhabitants on the island are Dr Moreau and his assistant Montgomery. Prendick imagines the animals to be human beings made bestial by Moreau's experimentation, but eventually he learns that they are animals to whom cruel but skilful vivisection and grafting have given a semblance of humanity, including the power of rudimentary speech. These 'Beast Folk' are Moreau's failures, sent back into the jungle and supposedly rendered harmless by his 'Law', which forbids them all predatory activity. But when one of the Beast Folk tastes blood, all hell breaks loose, particularly for Prendick.

KIPPS

♦ 1905 ♦

The engagement between Artie Kipps and the socially superior Helen Walshingham (right) proves to be short-lived. Kipps starts out as an unprepossessing young draper's apprentice and plunges even further down the social scale when he loses his job. His life is transformed, however, by an unexpected inheritance. He is taken up by Helen, but his adventures in genteel society constitute a series of painfully funny disasters. Eventually he flees and marries his first sweetheart, but fortune has not yet finished with him.

THE INVISIBLE MAN

♦ 1897 ♦

The scientist Griffin is a man without scruples (below). His bandages conceal his invisibility – his own brilliant discovery – and he is now frantically searching for an antidote. But when funds are short he feels no compunction about turning to crime. He burgles the local vicarage, flees and later returns to terrorize the villagers. Despite his invisibility he is wounded and takes refuge with a doctor Kemp. Kemp, however, calls the police. The tables turn as Griffin, thirsting for revenge, pursues and finally catches up with Kemp.

Mary Evans Picture Library

Stuart Lloyd: Beside the George and Dragon. Anthony Mitchell Fine Paintings/Fine Art Photographic Library

Universal/Kobal Collection

TONO-BUNGAY

♦ 1909 ♦

A primitive aircraft (rig provides a means of esca for the bankrupted Edw Ponderevo. Having mad and lost, a fortune with worthless patent medici Tono-Bungay, Pondere is threatened with prosecution for fraud. H nephew George comes t rescue. George is enamoured both of the infant science of aeronau and of his childhood sweetheart, a certain Beatrice Normandy. Beatrice, however, hints mysterious obstacles to their union. When Georg desperate attempts to he his uncle fail, he flies Ponderevo out of the country. But conditions the primitive aircraft pro too much for the older man, who subsequently dies of exposure. George left to rebuild his fortune and to discover the truth about the elusive Beatric

THE HISTORY OF MR POLLY
◆1910◆

A riverside inn (left) provides a temporary haven for Alfred Polly. Mr Polly is eccentric, imaginative and, at 37, at the end of his tether. Desperate to end his life and escape his wife Miriam, he sets fire to his house. But instead of dying he becomes a hero by rescuing an old woman from the flames. Soon afterwards he runs away and eventually finds contentment working and living at the riverside inn. But his conscience forces him home to see how Miriam is managing without him . . .

ANN VERONICA
◆1909◆

Radical and determined, Ann Veronica Stanley (below) is at loggerheads with her Victorian-minded father. She leaves home and takes lodgings in London, but learns that she cannot gain freedom without economic independence. A compromise arrangement with her father allows her to study biology at Imperial College. Here she falls in love with one of the teachers, Godwin Capes, a married man. They elope, scandalizing everyone.

Fine Art Photographic Library

Victorian notions of science as the key to infinite progress gave birth to a new literary genre. But soon the fiction began to question human competence to control the forces of technology.

The fiction of strange encounters is as old as literature itself, but with the Victorian boom in technology and science came a new kind of story – a genre that explored the seemingly limitless bounds of human knowledge. Victorian self-confidence gave way to doubts, however, and the greatest doubter – and the greatest visionary – was H. G. Wells. Ironically, his anxieties made, and made way for, some of the best science fiction of all.

As a literary form, science fiction has a mixed reputation. It is variously described as futuristic, escapist or visionary, as cheap pulp or prophetic mysticism. This is only natural with a genre that takes so many diverse forms. Some of its elements date back to the dawn of storytelling. The idea of travel far afield and of encounters with strange people and strange customs is even present in Homer's *Odyssey*. This ancient epic poem takes its hero far from known shores where he encounters monsters, suffers supernatural disasters and even quarrels with the gods themselves.

Another common element in science fiction is the 'alternative society' with a better or worse lifestyle than our own. Such fictional societies have often been used as a rich source for satire. Samuel Butler created his distant realm of *Erewhon* to hold 19th-century England up to ridicule. And Jonathan Swift had previously attacked the folly of his age in *Gulliver's Travels* (1726), through his fantastic islands of Lilliput and Brobdingnag, Laputa and Houyhnhnmland.

To the world's end
When the Mediterranean was the centre of the world, the classical journeys of such heroes as Ulysses constituted the ancient equivalent of science fiction. The stories featured strange creatures such as Sirens and storm nymphs in distant and unexplored tracts of ocean (left), born of half-believed sailors' yarns and an amalgam of cultural myths.

Frenchman with panache
Witty satirist and swaggering, stylish romantic, Cyrano de Bergerac (1619-1655) recounted visits to the Sun and Moon in order to make pointed comments about contemporary society.

*La terre me fut importune,
Je pris mon essort vers les Cieux,
J'y vis le Soleil et la Lune,
Et maintenant j'y vois les Dieux.*

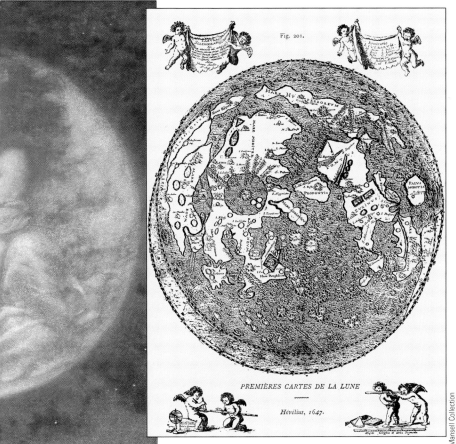

Fig. 201.

PREMIÈRES CARTES DE LA LUNE

Hévélius, 1647.

Mansell Collection

about Cyrano, staged in 1897, and incorporating his anti-gravitational theories, would almost certainly have been known to Wells.

Daniel Defoe (1660-1731), the author of *Robinson Crusoe*, also wrote about 'Worlds in the Moon', with a similarly satirical intent. And the 17th and 18th centuries kept up a steady flow of stories focused on other worlds. They were fiction, but they were not science fiction in the true sense, for there was no attempt at rational or scientific explanations. Travellers were driven off course by storms, borne on wings, or carried to their destination in dreams, like Dante conducted by spirits on a guided tour of the *Inferno* (Hell). Ebenezer Scrooge, that Dickensian traveller through time and space, is within the tradition of Dante and Defoe.

During the 19th century, the phenomenon arose that was vital to the creation of a new literary form: the growth of science and technology. The West's increasing affluence and domination of world trade were aided by new discoveries and technical ingenuity. It seemed that science would soon solve all problems, answer all questions.

Darwin's evolutionary theories also fired the fertile imagination. What if there were beasts which had evolved differently, in isolation, or had not become extinct (as in Conan Doyle's *Lost World* of dinosaurs)? What if Man's evolution took him beyond his present state and into some super-human form? What if Man could interfere

The Moon, tantalizingly close and yet inscrutable and unexplored, has always been the first resort of fantasy writers. As early as the second century AD, the Greek Lucian of Samosata wrote two extraordinary accounts of journeys to the Moon: *Icaromenippus* and *The True History*, translated into English in 1634.

When, in 1647, the astronomer Hevelius mapped the Moon, he gave rise to a flurry of fiction describing its supposed exploration by travellers. At the time, such stories were about as incredible as the voyages around the world of Ferdinand Magellan and Francis Drake.

FLIGHTS OF FANCY

Cyrano de Bergerac, the French poet, playwright, duellist and soldier, wrote an account of space travel, entitled *A Comical History of the States and Empires of the Moon* (1656). His aim was to satirize contemporary society by a description of lunar communities, but Cyrano also proposed (tongue-in-cheek) seven ways of reaching the Moon. He suggested anointing himself with morning dew and rising on its evaporation; greasing himself with the horn-marrow of beasts sacred to the Moon goddess; building a rocket fuelled with saltpetre; using a smoke-filled balloon; sitting on a metal plate and throwing a magnet repeatedly over his head; sealing up rarefied air in a 20-sided space capsule; and lying, wet-haired, head-on to the moonbeams when the Moon's influence on the sea was at its greatest. Edmond Rostand's play

Moonshine
Man's fascination with the Moon invested it with strange occupants and magical properties for thousands of years (above left). Hevelius' mapping in 1647 (above) encouraged lively speculation and much satirical fiction. But not until the Victorians envisaged going there was true science fiction born.

Kingdom of wise men
Jonathan Swift's Gulliver's Travels *includes an encounter with the flying island of Laputa (right). His purpose was not to excite the imagination so much as to provoke debate. His 'alternative society' was a vehicle for social satire.*

Mansell Collection

Jean-Loup Charmet

with the natural process of evolution? A new kind of writer awoke to the amazing possibilities.

When Edgar Allan Poe, as a young journalist, began to write a story of a journey to the Moon, he dismissed as fancy the efforts of Cyrano and the rest. His intention was to be as scientific as possible. The object was not satire but plausibility, and it appeared in 1836 under the title *The Unparalleled Adventure of one Hans Pfaall*.

Sir John Herschel set out to observe the southern hemisphere with one of the largest telescopes in the world, and there was every expectation that it would unmask all the Moon's secrets. Not three weeks after Poe's story appeared, a series of articles were printed in *The New York Sun*. They purported to be based on *The Edinburgh Journal of Science*'s coverage of Herschel's discoveries. Later, these articles came to be known as *The Great Lunar Hoax,* for they detailed vegetation, animals, intelligent life forms and cities, all supposedly sighted through Herschel's telescope. They caused a stir similar to that created by Orson Welles' 1938 radio broadcast of *The War of the Worlds.*

VERNE'S VOYAGES

Jules Verne (who hero-worshipped Poe) barely scraped a living writing articles and stories until, in 1863, he began a series called *Voyages Extraordinaires* – accounts of imaginary journeys into the unknown. *Five Weeks in a Balloon* (1863) reads like a factual record, akin to Henry Morton Stanley's dispatches from darkest Africa. Verne was the prime exponent of 'pseudo' scientific fiction. To strengthen his case, he packed his books with elaborate references to facts and figures and the latest scientific discoveries. His readers were enthralled. Verne's journeys took his readers to the North Pole, then to the centre of the Earth, and, having exhausted the Earth's potential, he turned to other worlds.

In *From the Earth to the Moon* (1865), he approached the problem of escaping Earth's gravity with great seriousness, and his novel reaches its climax in the launch of a giant bullet and its voyage around the Moon. He was not so foolish

Twentieth-century war?
The new century held out the prospect of unprecedented scientific advances. But what form would these take? Writers and artists began to speculate (above) – at a fantasy level.

Rodney Matthews

as to allow it to land there. He feared losing his scientific reputation by speculating about the surface of the Moon and then being proved wrong. His characters simply observe that the surface of the Moon is not habitable, and that any life form must inhabit the interior cavities – a theory taken up by H. G. Wells in *The First Men in the Moon* (1901).

Verne laid the foundation of the science fiction genre. His stories were thrilling, informative and optimistic of human progress through scientific advances. He wrote at a time when Victorian self-confidence was at its peak, but there were voices preaching caution even then. The Romantic movement mistrusted the tendency for science and industry to exploit and detach human beings from Nature. Mary Shelley's *Frankenstein* (1818) is the first science fiction story in which the wonders and horrors brought about by technology gallop out of the control and comprehension of the scientist who instigated them.

GLOOMY PREDICTIONS

As time passed, Victorian certitude gave way to the uneasy restlessness of the Edwardians. H. G. Wells, while writing in much the same vein as Jules Verne, added a new (or rather an old) dimension to the genre. He recaptured the element of social criticism present in those early satirical fantasies. An internationalist writing in an age menaced by militarism and jingoism, he told science-based adventure stories but used them to question the accepted values of contemporary society and of science.

Danger and derring-do
Author Jules Verne took readers 20,000 leagues under the sea (above), to the centre of the Earth, round the world in 80 days, and to the Moon and back. On every trip, life-threatening dangers beset his heroes. He gave his public well-constructed plots, humour, pace and, above all, detailed and credible futuristic technology – little wonder Verne won such a following among Victorians.

lished a formula for science fiction novels which was aped for many years afterwards. The story would begin with a discourse among gentlemen in which the feasibility of some invention was discussed, and after that the narrative of the adventure would be interspersed with large chunks of theory and/or philosophy.

When the possibility of travel to other planets was originally debated, it was envisaged that the inhabitants would either be like us or comically primitive and exploitable – not unlike those foreign 'savages' the Empire undertook to 'civilize'. It needed the post-Victorian mentality of H. G. Wells to suggest that the Earth could be visited by super-human life-forms and treated with the same disregard as 'civilized' Victorians treated lesser species and primitive cultures.

MARRED MIRACLES

Wells, for all his uncanny foresight, was the product of his time. In him a typically Victorian wonder at science was mixed with Edwardian fear of his fellow men's incompetence to put this science to good use. He chose not to turn his back on the future (as the Romantics had done), nor to reject the past (as the Modernists who dedicated themselves to a new age built on speed, power, design and mechanization did).

Wells' uncomfortable position, straddling the turn of the century, is best expressed in his masterpiece *The Invisible Man* (1897). The story is in the Gothic tradition of Mary Shelley, but is developed as a logical and scientific nightmare. Griffin, the anti-hero who dismisses the common rabble because they cling to their ignorance and do not appreciate the wonders of science, is gradually cut off from that society by his self-made 'miracle'

Jean-Loup Charmet

Jules Verne
Thrilling, epic and just plausible, the fiction of this brilliant Frenchman captured a young readership brought up in the Age of Science.

His predictions were astounding, leaving aside his merits as a writer or philosopher. He foresaw aerial and chemical warfare, pollution, various machines of war, genetic engineering and the exhaustion of the planet's resources – long before the term 'ecology' was even coined. And he predicted the atom bomb with uncanny accuracy.

Between them, Jules Verne and Wells estab-

Jean-Loup Charmet

Art or pulp?
A magazine of the 1930s (left) illustrates the appeal of the gruesome and blood-curdling – elements which damaged the reputation of science fiction as legitimate literature. By contrast, Wells' The Invisible Man *(on the Belgian poster far left), for all its chilling power, has a philosophical element which raises it high above the lurid sci-fi which, at one stage, swamped the market.*

Rodney Matthews

Edgar Rice Burroughs
Burroughs started his writing career on Mars and, after plunging into the African jungle, explored the Earth's centre and the Stone Age. He was a master of Fantasy (left) and one of the first of the American school which made sci-fi pay. His fiction often appeared alongside that of H.G. Wells and Jules Verne, serialized in the earliest specialist magazines.

Under a cloud
The menace of The Bomb (below) hung over science fiction for decades. Wells foresaw it, and its eventual use put an end to many writers' hopes that human wisdom would evolve as fast as technology.

of invisibility. He loses not just his visible body but his very self, finally cursed, cast out and hunted. Clearly the moral of the tale is that science should not be separated from society, nor trusted as an infallible answer to its problems.

THE SHIFT TO AMERICA

World War I proved Wells' visionary doubts more thoroughly than even he could bear. In the course of it, the tanks and the widespread mechanical destruction he had imagined became a horrible reality. In Britain, the effect was a waning of public interest in science fiction. Immediately after the War, any wish to think about the future gave way to a hedonistic obsession with the present. This was not so in the United States, however, where the public's fascination with and confidence in the future had barely been dented.

In 1919 Harold Hersey edited, in New York, *The Thrill Book,* a magazine which ran for 16 issues, mixing science and adventure. Then, in 1926, the first magazine devoted entirely to science fiction was published by Hugo Gernsback. It was called *Amazing Stories* and drew, at first, on European authors such as Jules Verne and H. G. Wells. But it also gave a creative opportunity to young American authors (and artists), the most notable being Edgar Rice Burroughs, the author of the *Tarzan* stories.

Gernsback relinquished control of *Amazing Stories* and became involved with the twin magazine *Science Wonder Stories* (which popularized the term 'science fiction') and *Air Wonder Stories.* Under the amalgamated titles of *Wonder Stories* these competed for readership with the rival *Astounding Stories.* Unfortunately, in the scramble for higher and higher circulation figures, the style degenerated into the era of the 'bug-eyed monster', the nasty alien. Travellers venturing boldly outwards from Earth invariably encountered

strange and grotesque beasts. When, in time, the astronomers proved that no other planet or satellite within the solar system was likely to support the life of earthlings, the pattern changed in favour of extra-terrestrials visiting Earth.

During the 1920s, the United States purveyed a progressive attitude to science; children raised on a diet of the amazing, the astounding and the wonderful, imbibed a notion that human potential was unlimited and invulnerable. Computers would enlarge the brain infinitely. Robots would serve and protect human beings. It took the Wall Street Crash of 1929 to crack American self-confidence, as World War I had undermined that of Europe. Across the Atlantic, the dark image arose of science as a dehumanizing agent; and in Europe, Aldous Huxley was writing the chillingly pessimistic *Brave New World* (1932).

A secondary reaction in literature to dire world events was the expansion of escapist fantasy. *Superman, Flash Gordon* and *Buck Rogers* formed one answer to the public's need to avoid grim reality.

Thus the elements of modern science fiction developed to include superficial, flashy escapism, the prophetic, futuristic vision and social satire. Those who inherited Wells' mantle include Isaac Asimov, Brian Aldiss, Stephen Leacock and George Orwell. And the implications of their writing still need to be taken as seriously as the significance of Wells' *Invisible Man.*

Popperfoto

W. SOMERSET MAUGHAM

◆ 1874 - 1965 ◆

A succession of grim early experiences drove Maugham to conclude that Life has no logic to it – no intrinsic meaning. He decided, therefore, to make the most of his talent while enjoying himself to the full. He was medic and bohemian, playwright and novelist, ambulance driver and spy – even his sex life was a search for variety. Although the critics dismissed his work, his readers disagreed, rating him the world over as the supreme storyteller, talented, versatile and engrossing.

EXILED IN SPLENDOUR

**Escaping England's confines and strictures,
Maugham settled in the South of France to a
life of opulence.**

In *The Summing Up*, written in 1938, Somerset Maugham looked back on his life and at the obstacles he had had to overcome. "I had many disabilities. I was small, I had endurance but little physical strength; I stammered; I was shy; I had poor health." But he also "somewhat early . . . made up my mind that, having but one life, I should like to get the most I could out of it." And this he accordingly did, travelling all over the world in search of adventure.

Chère Maman
Renowned for her sweetness and good looks, Edith Maugham (left) had 'an air of romance and tragedy about her', an impression which she unfortunately fulfilled. Always frail, she died of tuberculosis six days after William's eighth birthday. He treasured her memory and kept her portrait in his bedroom until the day he died.

William Somerset Maugham entered the world on 25 January 1874 on the second floor of the British Embassy in Paris. By this quirk of being born on 'British soil', Maugham would be exempt from doing French military service. His father, Robert Ormond Maugham, was a solicitor attached to the Embassy, a man renowned both for his kindness and for his ugliness. Maugham's mother, Edith Mary, was small, over 20 years younger than her husband and as beautiful as he was ugly. They were known, affectionately, as 'Beauty and the Beast', and Maugham's earliest memories of the two of them were almost painfully happy ones.

Born into an upper-middle-class family, Maugham lived in considerable comfort and style. Although he was the fourth son in the family, his brothers were at boarding school much of the time and Maugham often thought of himself as an only child. An imaginative and clever boy, he admired his father, adored his mother, and then suddenly, just after his eighth birthday, his happy world came to an abrupt and traumatic end. His mother, frail from tuberculosis, died after giving birth to a fifth child, who also died. And then two years later, in 1884, Maugham's father died 'of cancer

On British soil
Maugham's life began in relative opulence in Paris (below) on 25 January 1874, born to a lawyer father and society mother; the venue was the second floor of the British Embassy (below left). By being born on what was legally deemed British soil, Maugham and others like him would later be exempted from doing French military service.

Canterbury schooldays

From 1885 to 1889 Maugham was a boarder at King's School in the grounds of Canterbury Cathedral (left). Founded in the fifth century, it was the oldest school in England but its proud history was of little consolation to Maugham. He missed his parents, felt rejected by his uncle, and isolated from the other boys by his stammer. He was a good student, however, and came first in his class in 1886.

He escaped from the meanness of the vicarage by becoming a boarder at King's School, Canterbury; but this proved an even worse fate. William hated it. He was bullied mercilessly and mocked for his stammer and his ineptitude at games. Missing his mother, he threw himself into his studies with the hope of going to Cambridge later. But his health was poor. His mother and her sister had both died of tuberculosis, and when, aged 16, it was found that William's lungs were affected, he was sent to the south of France to recover.

IMPROPERLY EDUCATED

The loss of a year's schooling prevented Maugham from going straight to Cambridge, a matter which he later deeply regretted. Because of it, he never considered himself "properly educated". He harboured ambitions to be a writer, but he dared not voice them because writing was not a suitable occupation for a gentleman. Postponing a decision, he went to live for nine months in the German city of Heidelberg, and for the first time "tasted freedom" and "felt myself a man".

Free after eight years of misery, Maugham began to enjoy life. He attended lectures on philosophy and literature at the university. He learned to speak German fluently and was captivated by the cosmopolitan atmosphere of the city, so different from the stuffy, respectable life he had known in England. In Heidelberg he also met Ellingham Brooks, a Cambridge graduate and aspiring poet who was to become a lifelong friend, and with whom Maugham had his first homosexual liaison.

With £150 a year left to him by his father, Maugham felt himself to be independent, although the income was not enough for him to live the life of a gentleman. A career had to be

and grief'. Like his fictional counterpart in *Of Human Bondage,* the desolate boy was despatched to England to live with an uncle, the Reverend Henry MacDonald Maugham, vicar of Whitstable in Kent, and his German-born wife. According to Maugham his uncle and aunt were a joyless couple, strict, stern and penny-pinching. Already in their fifties when Maugham went to live with them, they were childless and seemingly insensitive to the boy's needs. Maugham spoke little English. He was desperately unhappy and developed a stammer which he was never able to master. Like Philip Carey's club-foot in *Of Human Bondage,* Maugham's speech impediment was a lifelong source of humiliation.

The vicarage

After the warmth and comfort of Paris, the vicarage (below right) in Whitstable, Kent, seemed a harsh substitute. Maugham's aunt and uncle were elderly, childless, set in their ways and ill-equipped as foster-parents. Maugham, then aged ten (below left), was painfully aware of their limitations and petty meannesses.

Key Dates

1873 born in Paris

1882 mother dies

1884 father dies; sent to Whitstable

1892 studies at St. Thomas's Hospital

1914 joins Red Cross; meets Gerald Haxton

1915 Liza born; *Of Human Bondage*

1916 marries Syrie Wellcome

1919–26 world travels

1927 divorces Syrie

1928 buys Villa Mauresque

1940–46 lives in US

1944 Haxton dies

1965 dies at Cap Ferrat

chosen. Returning to Whitstable he rejected his uncle's proposal that he enter the Church. He tried accountancy for two months and loathed it. A local doctor suggested medicine. Maugham felt no sense of vocation but agreed, excited by the prospect of living in London. Accordingly, in 1892, he entered St Thomas's Hospital as a medical student.

In his spare time Maugham read extensively, went to the theatre, visited brothels and wrote plays which, in his own words, "delved ruthlessly into the secrets of the human soul". Unable to get his plays performed, he turned his hand to fiction. The very first novel he wrote, *Liza of Lambeth*, was accepted by Fisher Unwin. Published in 1897, it drew on his experiences as an obstetric clerk in the slums of Lambeth. The book was widely reviewed and sold well. Aged 23, Maugham qualified as a doctor, and then, with a £20 advance paid to him by his publishers, he abandoned medicine and began his career as a professional writer.

Spain beckoned. "I settled down in Seville, grew a moustache, smoked Filipino cigars, learnt the guitar, bought a broad-brimmed hat with a flat crown, in which I swaggered down the Sierpes, and hankered for a flowing cape, lined with green and red velvet." After about nine months Maugham returned to London where he continued to write plays, novels and short stories. Several novels were published but none had the impact of *Liza*. Although not well-off, Maugham cultivated the air of a gentleman. He dressed well,

James Webb: At Heidelburg/Fine Art Photographic Library

A taste of freedom
Maugham spent a carefree 18 months in Heidelberg (above), discovering literature, ideas, and love – in the person of John Ellingham Brooks. But he needed a profession, and in 1892 he became a medical student at St Thomas's Hospital (left).

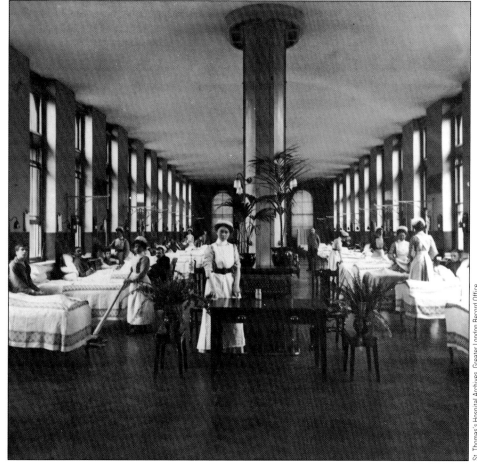

St. Thomas's Hospital Archives, Greater London Record Office

travelled widely and socialized with the rich. He spent weekends at the country house of the society hostess Mrs. G. W. Steevens, meeting other writers and artists. He shared a flat in Victoria with his friend Walter Payne, and conducted a number of brief affairs with Payne's discarded girlfriends.

EARLY DISAPPOINTMENTS
In 1903, Maugham's first play, *A Man Of Honour*, was staged in the West End, but it was a flop. He edited a literary magazine, *The Venture*, and when it failed, moved to Paris. There, at Le Chat Blanc restaurant, he met the writers Arnold Bennett, George Moore and Clive Bell. Here too he met the painter Gerald Kelly, an Irish old-Etonian who was later to become President of the Royal Academy and one of Maugham life-long friends.

With the failure of another novel, *The Bishop's Apron,* Maugham seriously considered giving up writing altogether and becoming a ship's doctor. But his fortunes soon turned – in 1907 his play *Lady Frederick* made him the most talked-about playwright in England, and within a year he had four plays running simultaneously in the West End. With his new-found wealth he bought a

house in London's Mayfair, and in 1909 became a member of the prestigious Garrick Club.

Maugham had always craved money and status. Having achieved both he was able to live life as he wished, but there was always a certain ambivalence in his attitude to the society to which he owed his success. Mercilessly exposing the hypocrisy of upper-class English society, Maugham was himself a living example of the double standard. Fastidious, courteous and conventional, he seemed a typical Edwardian man-about-town. He conducted numerous heterosexual love affairs but in private preferred men. With the trial and subsequent vilification of Oscar Wilde still fresh in his mind, Maugham was terrified of prosecution and kept his private life secret.

When War broke out in 1914, Maugham, now aged 40, joined a Red Cross ambulance unit in France. Serving in Flanders, he met a man who was to become the love of his life, the 22-year-old American Gerald Haxton. Haxton was an adventurer, dissipated and unscrupulous. As his relationship with Maugham developed he also revealed himself to be alcoholic, violent, dishonest and unfaithful. But according to Maugham's friend Glenway Wescott, their relationship was "the first completely beautiful, completely appropriate love affair Maugham had ever had". They were to stay together, first as lovers, then with Haxton assuming the role of secretary-companion, until Haxton's death in 1944.

Ironically, shortly after meeting Haxton, Maugham learned that he was going to be a father. He had met Syrie Wellcome, an elegant society woman, in 1911. She was married but separated from her husband, and for a while she and Maugham had been constant companions. On 1 September 1915 she gave birth to a daughter, Liza, Maugham's first and only child.

UNWILLING FATHER

Maugham had little desire to assume the responsibilities of a husband and father. When invited by Sir John Wallinger, head of British intelligence in France and Switzerland during World War I, to act as a link between London and agents in the field, Maugham readily agreed. Cited as co-respondent in divorce proceedings brought against Syrie by her husband, Maugham was out of the country before the case came to court.

In 1916 Maugham travelled to New York to arrange the production of his play *Our Betters*. Pursued by Syrie, he set off for Tahiti with Gerald Haxton to gather material for another novel, based on the life of the French painter Paul Gauguin, published later as *The Moon and Sixpence*. Returning to New York in 1916 he and Syrie married. Neither had any illusions about the other. Syrie knew of his homosexuality, he of her past lovers. Despite his fear of being trapped he felt honourbound to marry the woman who had borne his child; but Maugham had no intention of being a

War duties
With his knowledge of languages and training as a doctor, Maugham joined the Red Cross Ambulance unit (below) in 1914. He witnessed the ravages of war both in France and in Flanders.

Gerald Haxton
It was while with the Red Cross that Maugham met the handsome extrovert Gerald Haxton (left). A charming, dissolute American, he was to be the love of Maugham's life for the next 30 years.

SYRIE WELLCOME

Born in 1879, Syrie Barnardo was the daughter of the well-known philanthropist Dr Thomas Barnardo, founder of the homes for homeless and orphaned children. At 22 Syrie married the 48-year-old Henry Wellcome of Wellcome pharmaceuticals fame. When Maugham met her in 1911 she was separated from her husband and leading a hectic social life, courted by, among others, Gordon Selfridge of Selfridges department store. She had a child by Maugham – Liza – and was married to him for 11 years while Maugham flitted between her and Gerald Haxton. Although Maugham often maligned her, Syrie was a bright, talented woman who made a brilliant career for herself as an interior decorator.

Dangerous adventures

Maugham's and Haxton's boat capsized when journeying up the Sarawak River in Borneo (right). They nearly drowned, and Haxton suffered a heart attack.

dutiful husband and father. During the eleven years of their marriage Maugham was absent for much of the time, travelling abroad with Gerald Haxton. He felt he had little in common with his wife, regarded her career as an interior designer as socially demeaning and later complained to a friend, Glenway Westcott, that Syrie's "physical demands were intolerable, inexcusable".

After the anticlimax of his marriage, Maugham was again recruited into the ranks of British Intelligence. Armed with a large amount of gold, Maugham's mission was to buy off the Social Democratic government of Alexander Kerensky and keep Russia in the War on the side of the Allies. Maugham met Kerensky and was later to claim that, had he been sent to Russia six months earlier, he might have prevented the Bolshevik uprising. As it was, he was unable to elicit sufficient support to keep Kerensky in power. Soon after his return Maugham, with another bout of tuberculosis, entered Banchory Sanatorium at Kincardine, near Aberdeen in Scotland. During his three-months stay he wrote a play, *Home and Beauty*, and began making notes for his next novel.

FAME AND FORTUNE

With the end of the War Maugham entered into an intensely productive period. The success of *The Moon and Sixpence* in 1919 propelled him into being one of the best-known, most widely read and highly paid authors writing in English. At the end of 1919 he returned to the South Seas with Gerald Haxton, moving on to China, the Malay states and Indo-China before returning to the family home in London for a brief visit.

Throughout the 1920s Maugham's restless globe-trotting continued. In 1922 he visited the South Seas yet again. In 1923 he was in Ceylon and Burma and in 1924 Mexico, where he met D. H. Lawrence at a luncheon party. With a succession of box-office hits running in the West End – including *The Unknown, The Circle, East of Suez* and *Our Betters* – Maugham was now a rich man. In 1927 he and Syrie were officially divorced. Although they were in many ways unsuited to one another, Maugham's continuing relationship with Haxton was at the root of the divorce. Free again, Maugham bought a villa at Cap Ferrat on the French Riviera, where he was to live, apart from the war years, for the rest of his life.

Cap Ferrat is a peninsula which juts into the Mediterranean between Nice and Monte Carlo. In the Villa Mauresque, built by a Belgian King in the 19th century for one of his mistresses, Maugham wrote and entertained in style. In the years before 1939, house guests included the Aga Khan, the Duke and Duchess of Windsor, H. G. Wells, Arnold Bennett, Noël Coward, J. B. Priestley, Lord Beaverbrook, Winston Churchill and

Mary Evans Picture Library

Freddie Feest/Camera Press

Fine Art Photographic Library

Fact or Fiction

STARVING ARTIST

It is likely that Maugham had his brother Harry in mind when he created the character of Fanny Price. Fanny Price is a starving, unsuccessful artist who finally, in despair, hangs herself and is discovered in her squalid lodgings by Maugham's fictional counterpart, Philip Carey. Similarly Harry was an unsuccessful writer who in July 1904 poisoned himself with nitric acid. He lay in agony for three days before Maugham found him, but it was too late to save him.

Villa Mauresque
Maugham's home for 37
years was the splendid
Villa Mauresque near
Nice (below left). Here
he entertained family,
friends and royalty in
grand style. Maugham
was to sue his daughter
(seen below in the
swimming pool at the
Villa Mauresque with her
children) for the return of
all the gifts he had given
her. Meanwhile, he tried
to adopt Alan Searle, his
60-year-old secretary and
final companion as his son
(below right, dining with
Maugham in isolated
splendour).

Rudyard Kipling. There was a valet and maid for each guest, excellent food, tennis, bridge and nude bathing. The house was always full of books, flowers and handsome young men. Although mean in many ways – it was not until he was a very old man that he would pay for a taxi when he could use public transport – Maugham was a generous host and employer.

PAINFUL LOSS

Plays, short stories and novels, including *Cakes and Ale*, appeared at regular intervals. Many of Maugham's stories were made into films, and although critics considered the writer old-fashioned and out-of-touch with the times, the reading public continued to buy his work in ever-increasing numbers. Maugham was now 59 but had the energy and stamina of a much younger man. With Haxton at his side, he continued to travel widely.

When war broke out in 1939 Maugham remained at the Villa Mauresque until the Ger-

mans invaded France in May 1940. Knowing himself to be on Dr Goebbels' death list because he had helped to secure the release of Lion Feuchtwanger, a German Jew, from French detention, Maugham escaped to England on one of the last boats to leave Nice.

After five months in England, Maugham went to America in October 1940 to join Gerald Haxton. Deprived of his home and the freedom to travel, Maugham was given a modest house by his American publisher, Nelson Doubleday, in the grounds of his estate at Parker's Ferry, South Carolina. Maugham continued writing and toured America giving speeches in support of Britain's war effort. He saw little of Haxton who was working in Washington and drinking heavily. Although their relationship had deteriorated, Maugham remained deeply attached to him and was devastated when he learnt that his friend had TB. He spent a six-month vigil at Haxton's side, writing to another friend: "All the best years of my life were connected with him. . . . They say as one grows older one feels less; I wish it were true." Haxton finally died in November 1944. He was 52 years old – 18 years younger than Maugham.

For Maugham the pain continued. Bereft without Haxton, he wanted to die himself, but gradually, with the help of his nephew Robin and his new secretary Alan Searle, he started to improve. When the war came to an end Maugham returned to the Villa Mauresque accompanied by Searle, who was to remain his constant and faithful companion until Maugham's death.

SAFEGUARDING SECRETS

Known now as the grand old businessman of English letters, Maugham was lionized wherever he went. But public acclaim no longer satisfied him. The man who at 61 had looked "forward to old age" was not enjoying it. Panic-stricken that people should learn secrets about him after his death, he held nightly 'bonfires', destroying volumes of letters and documents relating to his life. In his will he left strict instructions that his executors should do nothing which might aid a would-be biographer.

Now in his late eighties, Maugham degenerated to the condition of his childhood, utterly dependent on Searle. As his long life drew to a close, he was consumed with bitterness. Never a kind or magnanimous man, his response to the misfortune of others was invariably "what the hell do I care?" In a series of sensational articles published in the *Sunday Express* in 1962, he told all, or almost all – hiding the essential fact of his homosexuality – about his dead wife, whom he portrayed as a malignant shrew. He tried to disinherit his daughter and adopt Alan Searle as a son. Having lost his physical faculties, Maugham finally lost his mind. On 8 December 1965 he fell in his garden at the Villa Mauresque and sank into a coma. On 15 December he died at the Anglo-American Hospital in Nice, six weeks short of his ninety-second birthday.

OF HUMAN BONDAGE

This semi-autobiographical novel mixes fact and fiction, drawing us into the plight of a boy, orphaned, crippled and isolated by loneliness, as he struggles to find a guiding philosophy.

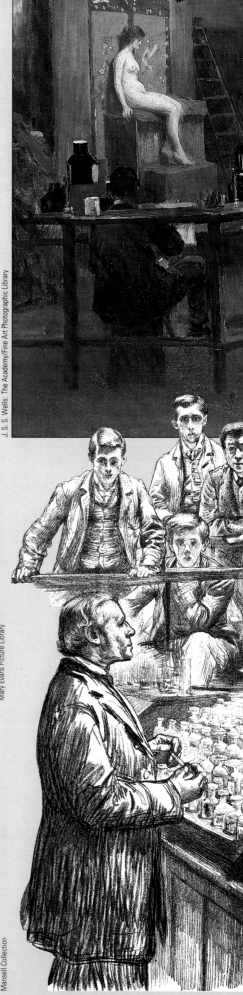

The best-known of Somerset Maugham's novels, *Of Human Bondage* is a stirring account of one young man's passage into adulthood. The anguish suffered by Philip Carey in his pursuit of love and adventure is heightened by being closely based on Maugham's own experiences. The richness with which Philip's character is drawn makes the story one of the most moving and engrossing of modern autobiographical novels.

GUIDE TO THE PLOT

Orphaned at nine, the frail, sensitive Philip is despatched to live with his childless aunt and uncle in Blackstable, a Kent-

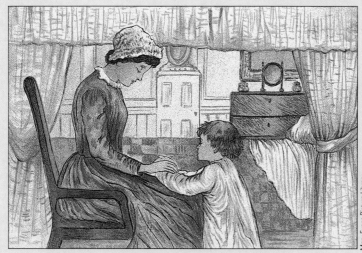

Sad farewells
Almost as painful for Philip as the death of his mother is his separation, shortly afterwards, from his beloved nurse (right). His uncle's insistence that he is too old for such an indulgence, and that "It costs too much money", is Philip's first lesson in the realities of life.

ish fishing village 60 miles from London. Philip's uncle is a selfish, parsimonious and narrow-minded vicar who has little interest in the boy. His aunt Louisa, however, longs to mother him, but a combination of shyness and knowing "nothing about children" makes her awkward and stiff in his presence. Isolated by a searing sense of loneliness, Philip feels the coldness and austerity of the vicarage deeply. Because playing is forbidden on Sundays, his aunt hands Philip some picture books, and so begins the boy's voyage into fiction and fantasy as an escape from the harshness of his world.

He is soon sent to board at Tercanbury Cathedral School, but this proves to be no improvement on the vicarage. Philip has a club-foot and the merciless bullying he has to endure on its account makes him "horribly sensitive" and unhappy. He retreats into his studies, but in spite of his academic successes he is desperate to leave school and experience 'life' as he imagines it. He goes first to Germany to study, and there mixes with an assortment of characters in Frau Professor Erlin's pension in Heidelberg. Returning home the following summer, Philip has his first love affair with the somewhat older Miss Wilkinson, but this too proves a disappointment. Her ardour soon embarrasses him and he unceremoniously flees.

Needing a profession, Philip takes up articles with a firm of chartered accountants in the City but is totally unsuited for the job. Quite against his uncle's wishes, Philip changes direction once again and, with his aunt's blessings and all her savings, sets off for Paris to study painting. Once there, he finds himself in the midst of a bohemian world which seems totally intoxicating.

Among his various fellow students is Fanny Price, an impoverished and talentless young Englishwoman. They strike up a friendship of sorts and later it is Philip who discovers her in her flat, hanged, driven to despair by poverty and failure. Shocked into reassessing his own life and confronting his lack of talent, Philip decides to give up painting. All around him are the drink-sodden wrecks of artists who discovered their mediocrity too late or never faced up to it.

60

Having squandered his aunt's savings and much of his inheritance, Philip returns to London and decides to train as a doctor. His studies are soon interrupted, however, by a chance encounter in a tea shop. He is attracted to Mildred, a waitress there, and her indifference to him only intensifies Philip's passion. He tries to buy her affections with the result that she comes to rely on him for money, appearing at his door whenever she is desperate. After a time Philip realizes he no longer loves her, but still cares too much to abandon her to the full horror of her fate.

Philip's life now takes an equally desperate turn when he plays the stock market and loses everything. He is forced to take a menial job as a shop-walker for six shillings a week, knowing the only event that could save him financially would be his uncle's death . . .

SELF-KNOWLEDGE
Writing *Of Human Bondage* helped Somerset Maugham to come to terms with his own feelings. As he explained in the preface, "*Of Human Bondage* is not an autobiographical novel; fact and fiction are inextricably mingled." In exploring and describing the emotions that had plagued his youth, he suddenly found himself "free from the pains and unhappy recollections that had tormented me".

> "He was troubled, and the fear seized him that love would pass him by. He wanted a passion to seize him, he wanted to be swept off his feet and borne powerless in a mighty rush he cared not whither..."

Philip Carey is a fictional character but the agonies he endures in learning to cope with the world into which he is born are clearly Maugham's own.

The language Maugham uses is plain and simple, and the structure is straightforward, starting with Philip as a young boy and ending as he reaches maturity. But the scope of the novel is immensely ambitious in its portrayal of one man's search for meaning. Every significant event of Philip's life is carefully chronicled with descriptions of his inner emotional life, so that he becomes intimately known to us. There is much that is universal in his experience of growing up, and a great deal of the pleasure to be had in reading the novel lies in the force with which we respond to the emotions that Philip is struggling with.

Paris studio
After a year at Heidelberg University and a brief spell back at Blackstable, Philip decides to try his hand at painting. He moves to Paris, enrols in art classes (above) and lives the life of a bohemian, complete with street cafés, art galleries and long, deep talks into the night.

Changing profession
Recognizing his lack of talent as a painter – "You will never be anything but mediocre" – Philip abandons his efforts before having to join the ranks of other ill-advised, destitute hopefuls. Medicine seems as good an alternative as any, and he enters St Luke's hospital in London (left) to start his new career.

RKO/Kobal Collection

Tea shop encounter
Philip's first impression of Mildred, the waitress in the tea shop (left), is that she is an "ill-mannered slut". But it is the beginning of his long, devouring obsession for her. In trying to help her he gets sucked into the vortex of her own self-destruction (above).

Beach and Palace Pier, Brighton.

himself seeking sympathy in ways that he does not understand: "He did things, he knew not why and afterwards when he thought of them found himself all at sea." Lonely and often friendless, he fantasizes that he is someone else:

"He would imagine that he was some boy whom he had a particular fancy for: he would throw his soul, as it were, into the other's body, talk with his voice and laugh with his laugh."

It takes him most of his early adult life fully to inhabit his own body and accept himself as he is. He moves from one occu-

Seaside resort
Three weeks after giving birth, Mildred and her baby go to Brighton (left), where the latest fashions, as well as sea air, beckon.

Struggling artist
Philip reveres Cronshaw (below), a brilliant and eccentric but penniless poet, who comes to a predictably tragic end.

A major part of Philip's journey to adulthood is spent learning about himself. He deals with the trauma of losing his mother and his nurse at a young age by developing a hard shell of apparent detachment. In his early months at the vicarage he falls asleep imagining he will wake up back at home with his mother. But waking just reinforces his misery and rather than crying in front of his aunt and uncle, he keeps it all bottled up, too proud to voice his wretchedness to them.

The greatest discovery Philip makes at this point is the world of books, but it is a double-edged pleasure:

"Insensibly he formed the most delightful habit in the world, the habit of reading: he did not

know that thus he was providing himself with a refuge from all the distress of life, he did not know either that he was creating for himself an unreal world which would make the real world of every day a source of bitter disappointment."

At school he finds the brutality of other boys an enormous shock. Used to spending long periods alone, he is suddenly catapulted into the violent world of the dormitory and classroom: "Philip passed from the innocence of childhood to bitter consciousness of himself by the ridicule which his club-foot had excited." It takes him many years to understand that when people want to hurt him they do so by mocking his deformity.

At school he is painfully shy and finds

pation to another with a restless yearning for something more, something better. He repeatedly finds himself with people with whom he can never be happy. His obsession with Mildred is inexplicable even to himself; he knows she will never return his love.

Gradually Philip discovers that he enjoys working as a doctor and that he has a certain skill in dealing with his patients. His friendship with Thorpe Athelny and his rambunctious family opens a new vista of possibilities for him: they like him as he is, despite his deformity.

THE MEANING OF LIFE

Maugham chose the title for *Of Human Bondage* to convey the sense of the futility of the human struggle in the face of material and spiritual poverty. Nearly everyone in the novel is trapped by the circumstances of their birth and the need for money.

In the Background

MEDICAL APPRENTICESHIP

Before the mid-nineteenth century the usual way to qualify as a doctor in Britain was to serve an unstructured apprenticeship to a surgeon or apothecary and then set up in practice. In 1858 the first Medical Act was passed establishing a General Medical Council to regulate entry to the profession. The Council decided what a modern doctor should know before being admitted to the Medical Register, and by the time Maugham trained as a doctor in 1892 the system combining practical work and exam was much as now, with practitioners separated into physicians, surgeons and apothecaries.

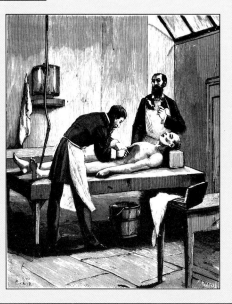

> *"...he chuckled: now that he had it, it was like one of the puzzles which you worry over till you are shown the solution and then cannot imagine how it could ever have escaped you. The answer was obvious..."*

Blossoming beauty
Philip's new acquaintance, Sally Athelny (left), "attracted because she was healthy, animal and feminine. She had many admirers", we hear, "but they left her unmoved."

Family hop-picking
It is when Philip joins the Athelnys on a hop-picking outing (below) that he finally sees in Sally a mixture of "a rosebud bursting into flower" and "some rural goddess".

Philip's determination to rise above the morass of seething humanity in pursuit of truth and beauty brings only more unhappiness. He finds himself asking endlessly what the point could be to such dissatisfaction and misery. Even love, which he believed would bring ecstatic happiness, is a source of acute suffering to him, "a bitter anguish he had never known before".

On his return from Paris, Philip sets about trying to understand his world by reading, but decides "Why the world was there and what men had come into existence for at all was as inexplicable as ever." Cronshaw, given to late-night philosophy in Paris cafés, tells him the meaning of existence lies in the intricate patterns of a Persian rug. The riddle remains unfathomable to Philip until much later.

His two years as a menial employee at Lynn's, the linen-drapers, convince him of the absurdity of life. He imagines suicide to be the best solution to his unhappiness. Sitting in the British Museum one day he asks himself desperately, "What did it all mean? He thought of his own life, the high hopes with which he had entered upon it, the limitations which his body forced upon him, his friendlessness, and the lack of affection which had surrounded his youth." Suddenly it comes to him – he realizes in a flash that it all means nothing. His life is of no more significance than any other. The weaver of Cronshaw's rug wove his patterns merely for his own pleasure. In the same way, everyone's life has a pattern, but its meaning is of no consequence.

All at once Philip sees his life differently; it does not matter that he has endured misery or that he may never realize his dreams: "Happiness mattered as little as pain. They came in, both of them, as all the other details of his life came in, to the elaboration of the design."

At last he is happy in his acceptance of life's arbitrary blows and prepares himself to make the best of whatever lies ahead.

CHARACTERS IN FOCUS

Of Human Bondage is filled with people and incident, and Philip Carey is one of the most involving heroes of modern fiction. It is his development, both intellectual and emotional, that forms the basis of the story and it is in relation to him that we view the other characters. His hunger to experience life becomes our hunger; and his joys and disappointments become ours.

WHO'S WHO

Philip Carey Acutely sensitive and shy, he longs for love, companionship and an exciting life.

Aunt Louisa "A little shrivelled woman", she tries to look after Philip as if he were her own son.

Mr Perkins The headmaster of Tercanbury School who impresses Philip and believes in him.

Hayward Pretentious, affected and idle, a Heidelberg friend with a romantic, literary vision of life.

Miss Wilkinson Having "somewhat the look of a bird of prey", she seduces Philip and is eager for more.

Cronshaw A philosophizing poet who "only comes out at his best when he's drunk".

Lawson "A thin youth with a freckled face and red hair", he is an intensely serious fellow artist.

Fanny Price A talentless, destitute art student whose hopeless situation ends in tragedy.

Mildred A common waitress who mesmerizes Philip to their mutual detriment.

Norah Nesbit A young, bright, cultured divorcee who genuinely cares for Philip.

Thorpe Athelny A true friend to Philip, he "talked inspiringly, with an eager vividness which fired the imagination".

Sally Athelny Thorpe Athelny's eldest daughter whose serenity saves the day.

With "a perfection of outline that took your breath away", **Mildred** (right) disgusts, captivates and obsesses Philip by turns. He first encounters her in a tea shop where she serves the customers with what seems a studied insolence. "She seemed to have a great deal of hair: it was arranged with peculiar elaboration and done over the forehead in what she called an Alexandra fringe. She was very anaemic. Her thin lips were pale, and her skin was delicate, of a faint green colour". Intrigued, Philip pursues her while she, secretly, is pursuing – and pursued by – another. Growing ever more involved in spite of her evident lack of interest, Philip tries to detach himself: "She was common. Her phrases, so bald and few, constantly repeated, showed the emptiness of her mind."

"A clergyman's daughter", **Miss Wilkinson** (left) "was a lady". "She wore a white muslin gown stamped with gay little bunches of flowers, and pointed, high-heeled shoes, with open-work stockings. To Philip's inexperience it seemed that she was wonderfully dressed." Entranced, he happily enters into a flirtation with her – an initiation into manhood which he later comes to regret.

An exuberant, eccentric journalist, **Thorpe Athelny** (right) first meets Philip as a patient suffering from jaundice. "He knew much more than Philip, both of the world and of books", and together they snatch moments of conversation, Philip revelling in the older man's passionate and picturesque expressions. Later, with boisterous enthusiasm, he welcomes Philip into the bosom of his family and proves to be his truest and staunchest friend.

The autobiographical main character, Philip (left) muddles his way through life's meandering course with a mixture of ingenuousness, shyness and youthful exuberance. Intent on unravelling the meaning of existence, he suddenly realizes there is none. And "if life was meaningless, the world was robbed of its cruelty. What he did or left undone did not matter."

John Byam Liston Shaw: When Love Came Into the House/Fine Art Photographic Library

Pierre Rivera: Le Bon Bock. Galerie George, London/Bridgeman Art Library

The holder of life's key, Cronshaw (right) proclaims that "life is there to be lived rather than to be written about." But he lives it too hard: "Sensual pleasures are the most violent and the most exquisite. I am a man blessed with vivid senses, and I have indulged them with all my soul. I have to pay the penalty now, and I am ready to pay."

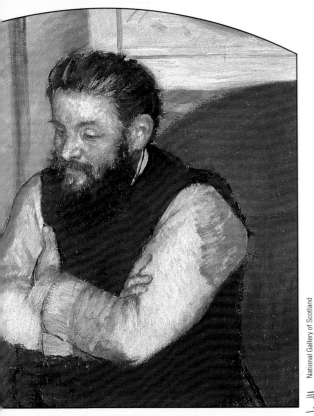

National Gallery of Scotland

A tired, timid and inadequate woman, Aunt Louisa (right) does her best to love and care for Philip. "In her tight black dress, made by the dressmaker down the street, with her wrinkled face and pale tired eyes, her grey hair still done in the frivolous ringlets of her youth, she was a ridiculous but strangely pathetic figure." She offers Philip her life's savings and he, with the selfishness of youth, accepts.

Mansell Collection

'TEEMING MEMORIES'

Possessed by the need to tell stories, Maugham bowed out of theatrical limelight in favour of the primeval fireside – to be the faceless storyteller speaking confidently out of the shadows.

Looking back on his work, Somerset Maugham, now in his sixties, commented, "I have a notion that I was more slow to develop than most writers." And indeed the majority of the novels and stories on which his reputation now rests were produced relatively late in his life.

After publishing a handful of novels as a young man – only *Liza of Lambeth* (1897) and *Mrs Craddock* (1902) are much read now – Maugham turned his attention to the stage, and in his thirties became one of the most popular playwrights of the day. His success was such that he "meant then never to write another book, but to devote myself for the rest of my life to the

drama." Even in old age Maugham believed that the 'slender baggage' he would carry with him into eternity – the works by which he would be remembered – would be just a handful of his plays and short stories. Curiously, he thought *Of Human Bondage* too long to find readers in later generations.

Although changes in public taste have made his melodramas seem dated, there are still revivals of Maugham comedies such as *Our Betters* (1917) and *The Circle* (1921). These are firmly in the long English tradition which he described as 'drama not of action but of conversation. It treats with indulgent cynicism the humours, follies and vices of the world of

fashion' – an attitude that Maugham found temperamentally congenial. His subjects, and the riches they brought him, gave Maugham a reputation for cynicism and commercialism that were to dog him throughout his career.

Despite his intention never to write another book, Maugham found that "I began to be obsessed with the teeming memories of my past life", which eventually "became such a burden to me that I made up my mind that I could only regain my peace by writing it all down in the form of a novel". The result was Maugham's return to fiction with an undoubted masterpiece, *Of Human Bondage* (1915), published when he was over 40. Although he was to write many more plays, he had entered a new phase – as a novelist and short-story writer – which would bring him an immense and enduring popularity.

Maugham's next works of fiction, the novel *The Moon and Sixpence* (1919) and the short story *Rain* (1921), sprang from the extensive travels that he now under-

...res convinced him that
...tial to an author's
...much so that he later
...rize to enable promis-
...to spend time abroad.
...anderings yielded sev-
...rt stories and the fas-
...s *On a Chinese Screen*
...an in the Parlour* (1930)
...(1935). Several of his
...*he Painted Veil* (1925),
...932), *Christmas Holiday*
...*r's Edge* (1944), are set

...US TRAVELLER
...d the anonymity of
...known 'gentleman in
...yside inn, and found a
...n of material in the Far
...ean planters, colonial
...d missionaries lived in
...al circumstances that
...eir own peculiar traits
...ve them to extremes of
...agerness with which

Success from sorrow
Liza of Lambeth was inspired by Maugham's work as a doctor in Lambeth (left).

Libellous likeness
The model for Kear in Cakes and Ale *was so cruelly and blatantly Maugham's friend Hugh Walpole (below) that Walpole wanted the book suppressed. He was placated, but the wound never healed.*

Scene stealer
The cartoon above shows Shakespeare sulking at Maugham's monopoly of the London stage: at one time he had four plays running simultaneously. Inset in the play bill (right) is a portrait of the rising star.

Maugham seized on their stories ("I have always worked from the living model") caused considerable resentment – in fact threats of libel action on the publication of *The Painted Veil* forced him hastily to change the location of the story and the names of his chief characters.

Maugham's sober, unromanticized view of human beings was sometimes regarded as positively unpatriotic, but for better or worse he fixed the image of the European in the Far East between the World Wars – especially that of the British man and woman in Malaya – as completely as Kipling had done a generation before.

FIRESIDE TALES
Maugham had little time for novels with a 'message' or for those written for propaganda purposes. His stated view of himself was deceptively straightforward: "As a writer of fiction I go back, through innumerable generations, to the teller of tales round the fire in the cavern that sheltered neolithic man. I have had some sort of story to tell and it has interested me to tell it. To me it has been a sufficient object in itself."

But although Maugham was not an experimentalist, constructing his novels and stories in traditional fashion with a beginning, a middle and an end, he developed his own strongly personal stance, tone and technique.

After *Of Human Bondage* he often wrote his fiction in the first person, creating a Maugham-like narrator who told what he

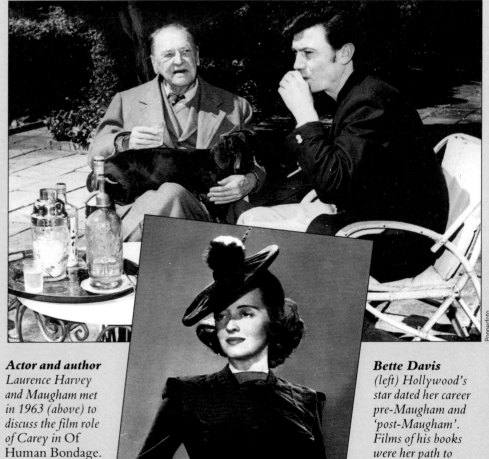

Weidenfeld Archive

"Success...
I don't believe it has
had any effect on me
. . . I always
expected it", wrote
Maugham (below).
Left, a revised page
of manuscript.

the most natural thing in the world. I took to it as a duck takes to water." But he also described himself as 'a made writer' who had worked hard to capitalize on his gifts of common sense and acute observation. Realizing that he had no talent for high-flying, he aimed for a style characterized by lucidity, simplicity and euphony (being pleasing to the ear). And although he founded his work on his observation of humanity, Maugham considered reality, undoctored and unrevised, a poor storyteller: "the artist does not copy life, he makes an arrangement out of it to suit his own purposes".

Maugham tells us this and much else in *The Summing Up* (1938), a classic account of a writer's development, methods and philosophy. It was penned when Maugham felt that he was approaching the end of his career, although he was in fact to publish several more novels and to branch out in his late seventies as an essayist of note. Despite his extraordinary commercial success, Maugham believed that what finally mattered was for the artist to satisfy his creative instinct. By doing so he escaped from 'human bondage', at least in his work. "The artist", asserted Somerset Maugham, "is the only free man."

knew of the main characters, partly through his contacts with them and partly through the gossip of recollections of other people. This enabled Maugham to restrict the story to what he allowed the narrator to witness or find out, so that episodes could be treated at greater or lesser length, the narrative could jump years at a time, and unexpected developments could be introduced with the maximum effect. Such was Maugham's skill that these devices are hardly noticed by the reader, who comes away with the impression that he has been reading a plain, absorbing tale – as Maugham intended.

'A MADE WRITER'

But more than technique was involved in Maugham's use of the first person. His narrator is everything that Maugham himself aspired to be – civilized, shrewd, without illusions, but infinitely tolerant of human frailty; his leisurely, reflected way of introducing himself, and his comments on people and events, give Maugham's fiction their utterly distinctive tone.

Maugham was capable of achieving something similar when writing in the third person, although it is significant that all three of his most highly rated later novels, *The Moon and Sixpence, Cakes and Ale* (1930) and *The Razor's Edge*, are told by an urbane narrator who is essentially the same person.

According to Maugham, "When I began to write I did so as though it were

Actor and author
Laurence Harvey
and Maugham met
in 1963 (above) to
discuss the film role
of Carey in Of
Human Bondage.

Bette Davis
(left) Hollywood's
star dated her career
pre-Maugham and
'post-Maugham'.
Films of his books
were her path to
fame.

Somerset Maugham's long literary career began when he was a medical student, and his first novel, *Liza of Lambeth* (1897), was based on the observations he had made while attending confinements in the slums of South London. After an interval, when he won fame as a playwright, he returned to prose fiction with *Of Human Bondage* (1915), one of the most influential autobiographical novels of the 20th century. The Tahitian background of *The Moon and Sixpence* (1919) was the first fruit of Maugham's extensive post-war travels, and many of his short stories dealt with the reactions of Europeans under pressure in the alien environment 'East of Suez', as in *Rain* (1921) and *The Painted Veil* (1925). *Ashenden* (1928) harked back to Maugham's own wartime experiences as a secret agent, and *Cakes and Ale* (1930) returned to the scenes of his youth in a mellower spirit than *Of Human Bondage*. Maugham continued to write novels until 1948, producing his last major work in *The Razor's Edge* (1944).

Mary Evans Picture Library

LIZA OF LAMBETH
+1897+

Liza Kemp, a girl of attractive vitality (above), is a product of the rowdy slum tenements of South London. She meets her fate when she performs a spontaneous dance to a barrel organ and is soundly kissed on both cheeks by a man with a beard. Later Liza and other locals go on an outing, and the man – Jim Blakiston – and his wife are among the party. Liza and Jim soon become lovers, but when Jim gives her a black eye after a quarrel their affair becomes public property. As a result, Jim's wife picks a fight with Liza in the open street and the girl is severely battered. When she returns home her mother 'cures' her with whisky. But their drunken hilarity subsides when it becomes clear that all is far from well with Liza – or with the child she carries inside her.

Gauguin Contes Barbares. Folkwang Museum, Essen/Bridgeman

THE MOON AND SIXPENCE
+1919+

The life of the great French painter Paul Gauguin inspired this novel about a middle-aged London stockbroker, Charles Strickland, who throws up his comfortable life to devote himself to art. Like Gauguin, he abandons his family and eventually settles in Tahiti (left). Strickland's dedication to art makes him ruthless in his personal relations, and in Paris he exploits Dirk Stroeve, a mediocre but good-hearted Dutch painter, and has an affair with Stroeve's taciturn English wife Blanche that results in her suicide. But 15 years later, when the unnamed narrator visits Tahiti, Strickland is dead. The narrator pieces together the painter's last years and a typically ironical Maugham ending makes the chief beneficiary of Strickland's genius the least appropriate of the book's characters.

RAIN
←1921→

Sadie Thompson, an American prostitute (left), is one of a group of travellers stranded by an epidemic on the rain-sodden island of Pago-Pago. They are forced to rent rooms in a seedy house, and Sadie is soon doing steady business. The others are morally outraged, and maddened by the incessant drumming of the tropical rain and the ragtime sounds from Sadie's gramophone. Davidson, a fanatical and repressed Scottish missionary, determines to make Sadie see the error of her ways, and a mixture of preaching and blackmail converts her. But Sadie is not the only person in the house at crisis point, and the climax of the story is surprising, shocking and bloody.

United Artists/Kobal Collection

THE PAINTED VEIL
←1925→

The divine Greta Garbo (right) starred in the film version of this story, one of Maugham's most incisive studies of human weakness.

In a darkened bedroom in Hong Kong, Kitty Fane becomes aware that a china knob on one of the shutters is moving. She and her lover, Charlie Townsend, panic, but nothing further happens. Nevertheless Kitty is rightly convinced that her husband Walter has found them out. Walter, a bacteriologist, tells her that he has volunteered to replace a dead medical missionary in a cholera-stricken Chinese town 30 miles away – and that he expects Kitty to go with him. When Charlie lets her down, Kitty has no alternative but to agree, although she is convinced that this is Walter's way of ensuring her death. Kitty's subsequent experiences of working at a French convent in the town and her growing respect for Walter's dedication significantly change her outlook. Then, ironically, it is Walter himself who succumbs to the epidemic. But on her return to Hong Kong, Kitty finds that there is more to face up to.

GARBO in THE PAINTED VEIL with HERBERT MARSHALL · GEORGE BRENT · WARNER OLAND · JEAN HERSHOLT · KATHARINE ALEXANDER · Based on the novel by W. Somerset Maugham · A Metro-Goldwyn-Mayer PICTURE

Directed by RICHARD BOLESLAWSKI PRODUCED BY HUNT STROMBERG

MGM/Kobal Collection

ASHENDEN
←1928→

Gentlemanly intrigue (left) features in the six stories in this book, which was based on Maugham's own experiences in British Intelligence during World War I. Ashenden, a successful writer, is recruited by 'R', who tells him that his knowledge of several languages will be useful, and that his profession will provide an ideal cover for intelligence work. Ashenden takes up residence at a hotel in Geneva where he plays bridge with rival agents and supervises undercover operations. One of them (in the story 'Giulia Lazzari') involves an Indian who is lured onto French territory by his Italian mistress, who loves him but is desperate to save herself.

Mansell Collection

CAKES AND ALE

◆1930◆

Rosie Driffield, with her sweet smile and ample blonde beauty (left), is Maugham's most enchanting heroine. Willie Ashenden is approached by his old acquaintance Alroy Kear who has been commissioned to write the official biography of Edward Driffield, the last of the great Victorian novelists. Ashenden had known him 40 years earlier and recalls his boyhood in Blackstable and his meetings with a not-yet-respectable Driffield and his ex-barmaid wife Rosie, a delightful, generous person who gave herself easily to men she found sympathetic.

THE RAZOR'S EDGE

◆1944◆

Larry Darrell (below) is a kind of modern saint. Returning to Chicago after serving in the First World War, he cannot settle down to marriage and a career. Reluctantly, his fiancée Isabel Bradley agrees that he should spend two years of self-education in Paris. When it becomes apparent that Larry will never make a 'proper' career, Isabel marries his best friend, Gray Maturin. But their imagined security vanishes with the Wall Street Crash, and Larry enters their lives again, having found enlightenment in India. When Larry tries to save a girl bent on self-destruction, the jealous Isabel takes horribly effective action.

SECRET AGENTS

Espionage was so unsophisticated at the time of World War I that a gentleman writer such as Maugham could be drafted into the Secret Service for missions of the highest importance.

In the preface to the short stories he based on his experiences as a secret agent Somerset Maugham wrote: "The work of an agent in the Intelligence Department is on the whole extremely monotonous. A lot of it is uncommonly useless." His involvement with espionage in World War I began in 1915, and he thus shared in the germination of British intelligence, which had existed only since 1909. The passage of time has made the true story of 1914–18 espionage hard to unravel. One

thing is plain, however: at times it served to change the course of history.

The Secret Service Bureau came into being between August and October 1909. The Home Section, MO5 (later MI5), had a staff of only 19 at the beginning of the War which had risen to 344 by the end. The Foreign Secret Service Bureau (later MI1C, then SIS) was born out of an exaggerated fear of German invasion. Spy scares were rampant – as witnessed by the passing of the Official Secrets Act in 1911. But the FSSB was built of only a handful of part-time agents and vied with the better financed, professional Royal Navy's Intelligence Division, and with spying diplomats. Neither branch could afford to pay staff adequately, so they relied on employing people

Pigeon post
Carrier pigeons – used in espionage since Roman times – were an important means of communication in World War I.

Novelist and spy
Like his friend Maugham, Sir Compton Mackenzie (code-name 'Z') worked for the Secret Service during the War.

with private incomes, rewarding them with immunity from income tax!

Karl Ernst's barber's shop at 402a Caledonian Road, London, had been known by MO5, since 1910, to be the 'letter box' for German spies. So on the day War was declared, all of the 21 known German agents in Britain could be rounded up. During the War several more agents entered the country, purporting to be neutral citizens. But they seldom evaded arrest for more than a few weeks and were shot or hanged according to their military or civilian status.

Although routine counter-espionage began early, everyone thought the War would be over by Christmas. So few countries were geared up for large-scale, long-term espionage. Only as winter saw the unbroken deadlock of trench warfare set in on both Western and Eastern Fronts were spy networks built up.

The French presented the British Intelligence Corps with its first 15 homing pigeons. These would be the prime means of communicating information from behind enemy lines before the advent of portable radios. The pigeons were tolerant of shell fire and did not succumb to poison-gas as readily as human beings. By 1916 three units of pigeon handlers served in the British Courier Service (Royal Engineers), and by the end of the War 20,000 birds had joined the War effort. The security threat to Austro-Germany was so great that any civilian caught in possession of a pigeon ran the risk of being shot.

Britain, France and Belgium agreed to set up a 'joint' intelligence bureau at Folkestone on the English south coast to process agents' reports arriving from occupied Belgium and neutral Holland. The British section was run, until 1917, by a former gunner, Captain Cecil Cameron, from a house on the seafront.

INCOMPETENCE AND BETRAYAL

But Cameron's was not to be the only spy network destined for the Low Countries. Major Walter Kirke, Deputy Head of Intelligence at British Expeditionary Force GHQ established the 'WL' network in April 1915. To organize the network, Kirke picked Major Ernest Wallinger, another gunner. The well-to-do Wallinger set up office in his Knightsbridge flat, near Harrods.

Wallinger, in turn, recruited his elder brother John, an Indian Police captain, who had lost a foot in one of the battles in 1914, to run operations in neutral Switzerland. The first Swiss network collapsed through a mixture of incompetence and betrayal. The British consuls in Swiss cities proved unreliable: closely watched by Swiss police, some were accused of spying and expelled. So in September 1915 John Wallinger recruited Somerset Maugham.

John Wallinger's mistress was a friend of Maugham's own mistress and future wife, Syrie Wellcome. But Maugham had more to recommend him than that. He spoke fluent French and German (in fact he wrote his first play in Ger-

man). He had private means and, as an unfit 41-year-old, was not likely to be conscripted. So, after one wartime career driving Red Cross ambulances on the Western Front, Maugham took up a second as a spymaster. Over in Greece, his flamboyant novelist friend Compton Mackenzie, under the code-name 'Z', received lavish funds to report to the fabled 'C' (Captain Mansfield Smith-Cumming RN, first chief of the Secret Services). By contrast, Maugham worked, unpaid, for a shoestring, temporary operation.

ESCAPE LINES

Maugham's first task was to lure into Allied territory an expatriate Englishman living in Lucerne and working for the Germans. To judge from his barely fictional short story 'The Traitor', he was successful. Once a week he crossed Lake Geneva to France to obtain London's instructions. An old woman – a vegetable-seller in the Geneva marketplace – acted as Maugham's courier.

But before December 1916, John Wallinger's Swiss network was closed down. Britain's spy agencies had decided to concentrate entirely on Holland, a nearer neutral country with laxer security. From here the Allies sustained crucial escape lines for prisoners-of-war and reported on train-movements in occupied Belgium. Nurse Edith Cavell, working in Brussels, helped scores of Allied servicemen escape, but was certainly not a spy. Her execution by the Germans on 12 October 1915 sparked worldwide outrage. Ironically, it later saved many genuine Allied female spies from the death sentence, as Germany did not dare risk more damage to its reputation.

By May 1916 the British-run 'Frankignoul' net-

A heroine's death
The nurse Edith Cavell was one of the greatest heroines of World War I – a model of courage and humanity. She was executed by the Germans for helping Allied soldiers to escape from occupied Belgium, and her killing greatly damaged the German reputation. The French illustration (bottom) shows how her death was used for anti-German propaganda.

Miss Edith Cavell

Jean-Loup Charmet

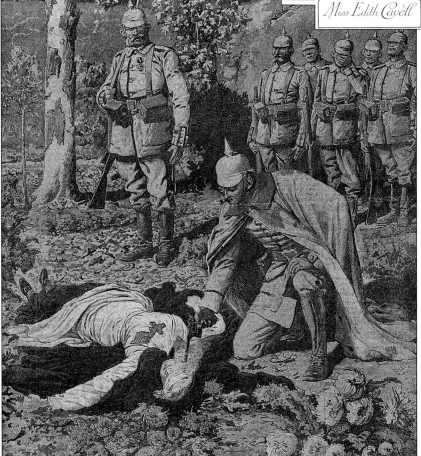

Sources and Inspiration

work totalled over 40 train-watching posts. But when reports were captured from the British steamer *Brussels* many arrests followed. The situation was saved by the 'Lux' espionage network organised by Belgian Catholic priests. They smuggled train-watching reports out by barge, past the double electrified fence built by the Germans along the Dutch border. In November 1917 'Lux''s prime-mover, Abbé Buellens, was finally arrested. But by then the even larger 'White Lady' (*La Dame Blanche*) network was in full operation, aided by MI1C. By Armistice, 'White Lady' had 919 agents reporting from 90 observation posts and provided 75 per cent of all Allied intelligence via neutral states.

DOUBLE AGENTS

Backing up 'White Lady', Wallinger had 11 small Belgian networks, three run by double agents. One, called 'Felix', was composed of prostitutes paid in cash and drugs. Thus British intelligence held sway over 5000 Belgian spies (seven times more than French and Belgian Intelligence combined). The Germans convicted 235 Allied agents – only three were British.

From as early as the autumn of 1915 agents were being landed in occupied territory at night by aircraft. Ten British-paid spies were even sent in by balloon early in 1917. The French parachuted agents into Alsace, and the Allies dropped them into occupied Serbia – as they would do again in World War II. Ingeniously, baskets of carrier pigeons were dropped behind the Western Front too, by parachutes released from a mini-balloon by an alarm-clock timing mechanism. Questionnaires printed in French and Flemish were clipped to the birds' legs in small aluminium containers. At least 40 per cent returned with messages, some within ten hours.

MATA AND MARTHE

German intelligence could never compete with Allied efforts. Mata Hari (literally 'The Eye of the Dawn') was the exotic alias of Dutch dancer Margaret Gertrude Zelle. She has gone down in history as the archetypal spy-seductress, but her career in espionage is obscure and controversial. In 1917 she was arrested in Paris and charged with spying for Germany. She claimed she was a double-agent, working for France against the Germans, but she was found guilty and shot by firing squad. She certainly had many military officers among her lovers, but whether she gained – and passed on – valuable information from them is open to doubt.

By contrast, Marthe Richard, a French war widow, was of inestimable value to the Allies. She volunteered to be an agent only three weeks after her pilot husband Henri's death in action. Multilingual and the owner of a pilot's licence, she became the mistress of the German naval attaché in Madrid reporting to Paris until 1918, as her memoirs, *I Spied for France*, recall.

Meanwhile, over in America, German money was financing a desultory programme of sabotage,

Temptation
Mata Hari (right) and Marthe Richard (below) used their undoubted sex appeal as weapons in the espionage war, but with different results: Mata Hari was executed, Marthe Richard became a national heroine. Before the days of sophisticated electronics, spies used devices such as the hollow bar of chocolate (above) for carrying messages.

which had no effect except to inflame pro-Allied feelings. A mere seven agents operated there after America's entry into the War. The meagre success of German espionage against her opponents in general is witnessed by the fact that its soldiers knew nothing of tanks, for example, until confronted with them on the battlefield.

THE EASTERN FRONT

It was a different matter in the East. Austro-German code-breakers were keeping effective tabs on Russian troop movements. In order to hasten capitulation of the already demoralized Russians, the German Foreign Office funded revolutionary propaganda. Their master-stroke was to ship Lenin and 32 other revolutionaries in a locked train from Switzerland to Petrograd (now Leningrad) via Sweden in April 1917.

In Petrograd a precarious Provisional Government was attempting to rule after the Tsar's abdication. Its Prime Minister was Alexander Kerensky, a brilliant socialist who had already served as Minister of Justice and War. Unlike Lenin and the Bolsheviks, he wanted to continue the War before transforming Russian society. But his summer offensive failed.

To sustain Kerensky and to prevent the feared Bolshevik coup, MI1C's man in the US, Sir William Wiseman, telephoned an old family friend –

Somerset Maugham – then staying in New York. Would he go to Russia and send back information for him. After 48 hours' deliberation Maugham accepted. This time he would be working for the regular British Secret Service, with both London's and Washington's blessing. Wiseman wrung $75,000 out of each for the mission. Maugham received the fabulous sum of $21,000 in salary and expenses, and sailed from San Francisco for Tokyo on 28 July.

A 10-day journey by Trans-Siberian Railway brought Maugham to Petrograd early in September. Through the British Embassy, and in his own secret code, Maugham promptly sent lengthy reports to New York. In them, he was able to name 'the chief German agent in Russia' as Max Warburg, a Hamburg banker.

'Somerville', as Maugham code-named himself, gained speedy access to Kerensky and wined and dined the Prime Minister or other members of government at the luxury Medvied Restaurant. By 24 September, 'Somerville' was reporting that 'Lane' (Kerensky) was losing popularity and changing his mind daily about whether to move to Moscow to avoid the Bolsheviks.

'Russia . . . is just being held together by English agents', wrote the German Foreign Minister on 29 September. He may have had Maugham in mind. On 16 October, Maugham cabled Wise-

Intrigue in Russia
In 1917 Maugham travelled to Russia on an important secret mission. After a journey on the Trans-Siberian Railway (top left) he met Alexander Kerensky (above), the Prime Minister of the second provisional government before the Bolshevik October Revolution, and reported back on the unstable condition of the country. Maugham's path was smoothed by Sasha Kropotkin (inset), whom he had known in London. The daugher of a Russian anarchist prince, she was a formidable woman who became the model for the femme fatale in one of Maugham's Ashenden *spy stories.*

man in Washington urging $500,000 a year to be spent on promoting the Menshevik (moderate socialist) cause, and on recruiting Poles, Czechs and Cossacks to counteract 'German plots and propaganda'. The Germans were only 250 miles from Petrograd, which at this time was the Russian capital. Then Lenin returned from Finland on 20 October to persuade his comrades to organize an armed uprising without delay.

MEETING WITH LLOYD GEORGE

On 31 October Kerensky summoned 'Somerville' and gave him a message for Lloyd George. There must be an immediate Allied peace offer 'without annexation or compensation', so that a German refusal would outrage the Russian Army into fighting through another winter. Second, the Allies must regularly supply guns and ammunition. Third, Allied newspapers must be more sympathetic to the new regime. Fourth, the reactionary British Ambassador must be replaced.

Maugham left Petrograd that evening, picking up a Royal Navy destroyer at Oslo for a rough crossing to Scotland. Next morning, having written down Kerensky's message for fear his stutter impair a spoken version, Maugham presented

himself at 10 Downing Street. Lloyd George read the account and replied, 'I can't do that', then promptly entered a Cabinet meeting. Forty-eight hours later, Lenin was in power and Maugham's secret service career was over.

As late as 1962 Maugham was still speculating; 'Perhaps if I had been sent to Russia six months sooner, I might have been able to do something . . .' In reality, no amount of money or espionage could have staved off the chaos which ensued. His practical achievements as a spy did not match the spectacular (if embroidered) feats of fellow novelists Compton Mackenzie or A. E. W. Mason. But his experience gave him invaluable material for those 16 *Ashenden* short stories and the 14 others he burnt because they infringed the Official Secrets Act.

Maugham was a conscientious agent, although the *Times Literary Supplement* concluded, upon reviewing his *Ashenden* stories, 'counter-intelligence work consists often of morally indefensible jobs not to be undertaken by the squeamish or the conscience-stricken'. Spy-novelist John Le Carré called Maugham 'the first person to write about espionage in a mood of disenchantment and almost prosaic reality'.

The Russian volcano
Maugham's visit to Russia in 1917 failed in its purposes: to persuade the Russian government to continue the War against Germany, and to prevent the Bolsheviks, led by Lenin (making a speech, above), from winning power. In the West the Russian Revolution seemed like a volcano erupting.

JOHN GALSWORTHY

1867-1933

Rebel, social reformer and, finally, an Establishment figure,
John Galsworthy was the quintessential English gentleman
who became the foremost writer of his day. In his chronicles of
the Forsytes, he mirrored both his own family and Victorian
and Edwardian conventions and manners. As a moral
campaigner, he fought against the injustices of society while
remaining fast entrenched inside it. 'He would go to the stake
for his opinions but he would go courteously raising his hat.'

MAN OF PRINCIPLE

Moulded by the manners of the upper-middle class, Galsworthy was placed 'beyond the pale' by his own behaviour and by his criticism of bourgeois complacency.

John Galsworthy called his fiction 'the criticism of one half of myself by the other'. Though he attacked the class he was born into, he never gave up its formidable privileges, and in time the rebellious young man became the personification of the very society he had condemned.

WEALTH AND STATUS

He was born on 14 August 1867 at Kingston Hill in Surrey, the second of John and Blanche Galsworthy's four children. His mother was by all accounts a rather fussy, narrow-minded woman, tolerated rather than liked by the family. His father, the model for old Jolyon in *The Forsyte Saga,* was a solicitor in the City of London who maintained lucrative business interests. Galsworthy idolized him – 'I was so truly and deeply fond of him that I seemed not to have a fair share of love left to give my mother', he wrote.

The family enjoyed the fruits of 'old' John Galsworthy's wealth in 'that moneymaker's Golden Age, the nineteenth century'. Shortly after Galsworthy's birth they moved to a large private estate at Coombe in Surrey, the original of Soames' grand home, Robin Hill. Galsworthy's father had no fewer than three houses built within the walled gardens of Coombe, and the family lived in them in rotation, while the young Galsworthy had the run of the pastures and woodlands of the estate. It was a privileged and idyllic childhood.

At the age of nine, Galsworthy went to Saugeen school in Bournemouth, and five years later, in 1881, to the famous public (private) school Harrow,

Out of town
Old John Galsworthy needed to live near London, but believed in bringing up children in good country air. Near Richmond (right), he built an ugly Gothic mansion called Coombe Warren (below) and two other houses. The family spent time at all three.

By permission of the University of Birmingham

By permission of the University of Birmingham

Ill-matched parents
Blanche Galsworthy (left), according to her son, 'had no speculation in her soul'. Conscious of having married beneath her, she was soon at odds with husband and family, tolerated rather than liked. John Galsworthy senior, however, inspired admiration and love. He is pictured right with his grandson, Rudolf Sauter, who was to become trustee of the novelist's literary works.

By permission of the University of Birmingham

Key Dates

1867 born in Surrey
1890 called to the Bar
1891-94 travels worldwide
1895 affair with Ada
1905 marries Ada
1906 *The Man of Property*
1911 affair with Margaret Morris
1916 serves in French hospital
1932 Nobel Prize
1933 dies, Hampstead

The foreign trips his father sent him on between 1891 and 1894 – to Canada, the South Seas, and Russia – did little to concentrate his mind, or cure him of his love for Sybil Carr, as old John had hoped. Indeed, though Sybil did finally fade from the scene, Galsworthy was now adamant that neither law nor commerce was right for him – 'It does seem to me so beastly dull to go on grinding at a profession or business just to make money', he wrote. It was at this time that his elder sister Lilian began to exert a liberating influence on him.

'WHY DON'T YOU WRITE?'

An intelligent and free-thinking woman, Lilian had grown sharply critical of her parents' values and assumptions. Through her Galsworthy began to question Christianity and to move towards the sort of compassionate, humanistic view of life that came to dominate his thinking. Lilian's marriage in 1894 to the painter Georg Sauter, the son of Bavarian peasants, further influenced him. It brought into the family fold the first person Galsworthy had met whose attitudes had not been shaped by an English upper-middle-class upbringing. For the first time Galsworthy considered the possibility of becoming a writer – a somewhat bohemian profession for someone of his class. 'I do wish I had the gift of writing. I really think that is the nicest way of making money going.'

Galsworthy's future wife, Ada, is credited with hardening this vague hope into a consuming ambition. She claimed that a throwaway remark by her at a Paris railway station 'gave the first impetus towards the literary calling of John Galsworthy'. Certainly Ada's influence – for good

where he had 'on the whole a happy time'. According to his headmaster he was 'a quiet, modest, unassuming boy' who 'made his mark both in work and play, without affording any notable promise of distinction in after-life'.

Indeed, when Galsworthy went up to New College, Oxford, in 1886 to read Law, he looked set on the sort of respectable career usually followed by the sons of the upper-middle class. He cared little for intellectual pursuits and was an indifferent student – his favourite pastime at Oxford was gambling on the horses.

FOR LOVE, NOT MONEY

By this time the family had moved into London, to Cambridge Gate on the edge of Regent's Park. Galsworthy divided his college holidays between Cambridge Gate and the country houses of Oxford friends, through whom he met and fell in love with a singing teacher called Sybil Carr. Although he was ardently attached to her, it was not a match that pleased his family.

Galsworthy left Oxford in 1889 with a second class degree in Law and was called to the Bar the following year. He was little suited to the law, however, and pursued it only to please his father – 'I read in various Chambers, practised almost not at all, and disliked my profession thoroughly'.

Harrow's athletic hero
John was head of house and captain of the House Football team (above). He was rated a capable pupil, although 'weak in composition'.

and ill – cannot be overestimated.

She and Galsworthy had first met at a family party to celebrate her marriage to Galsworthy's cousin, Arthur. It was a deeply unhappy marriage, one she had agreed to only in order to escape the misery of her unfortunate past (she had been born illegitimate), and she was soon confiding her

79

unhappiness to Galsworthy's sisters, Lilian and Mabel. The harrowing details of her marriage, as related by his sisters, excited first Galsworthy's compassion and, in time, his love. He and Ada began to meet in secret, and in September 1895, when Ada was 30 and Galsworthy 28, they became lovers.

His affair with Ada was to invite the stern censure of the English Establishment, obliging him to resign from his London club and the various directorships secured him by his father. But his love for Ada and his desire to compensate for the miseries of her past were profound. She repaid him with unstinting support for the writing career he decided on after giving up the law for good in 1895.

PERSONAL AND PUBLIC TRIUMPHS

Galsworthy's writing apprenticeship was slow and painful, his early efforts shallow and amateurish – 'For . . . eleven years, I made not one penny out of what I, but practically no others, counted as my profession', he recalled. He was fortunate in having as friend and mentor the influential critic Edward Garnett, then the centre of a group of up-and-coming writers.

It was Galsworthy's burning resentment of the way he and Ada were ostracized for daring to love one another that fuelled his best writing and found its most assured artistic expression in *The Man of Property,* published in March 1906. By this time old John Galsworthy had died, Ada had obtained a divorce from Arthur, and she and Galsworthy had married, after ten long years. The year 1906 marked a peak of artistic achievement for Galsworthy. The enthusiastic reception of *The Man of Property* – 'Book successful . . . excellent reviews',

New College, Oxford
Galsworthy went up to Oxford (above) to read Law in 1886. He was remembered as 'the best dressed man in College . . . withdrawn, saying little, a sensitive amused, somewhat cynical . . . spectator'.

he noted – was followed up by the success of his stage play *The Silver Box,* which closed on a note of triumph in 1907 when the Prince and Princess of Wales attended the last night's performance.

The Galsworthys spent much of their time together on the move, from London to the Devon farmhouse, Wingstone, that Galsworthy loved so much, to Littlehampton and, in the winter, Italy, the south of France or further afield. This itinerant lifestyle was largely for the benefit of Ada's

ADA AS IRENE

Irene in *The Forsyte Saga* is modelled on Galsworthy's wife. Ada's attempt to escape her mistaken marriage to Major Arthur Galsworthy is reflected in Irene's doomed love for Bosinney. The author assuaged his sister's worries about fictionalizing this episode by saying, 'who really knows enough or takes enough interest in us . . . to connect A with I, especially as I have changed her hair to gold?' He was wrong, of course. Arthur Galsworthy was branded a brutish, Soames-like tyrant – possibly a rapist (as Ada certainly portrayed him). But general opinion knew him for a quiet, pleasant man with a consuming interest in the army.

health. She suffered from asthma and rheumatism and became increasingly sickly after their marriage. Galsworthy nursed her devotedly. They were a very private couple, rather stiff and formal with all but very close friends, and they could not easily forget how society had shunned them.

Nevertheless they were rapidly becoming public figures and Galsworthy began to support a variety of causes in accordance with his passionate beliefs. Always a sensitive soul, distressed by the slightest suffering – whether human or animal – he wrote a flood of articles on issues as diverse as the censorship of plays, women's suffrage, the docking of horses' tails and pigeon shooting.

CAMPAIGNS FOR REFORM

The most successful of these campaigns concerned the practice of solitary confinement in prisons. From his Devon farmhouse Galsworthy made, in 1907, the first of several visits to Dartmoor Gaol and during the next two years completed a rigorous schedule of prison visits throughout the country. His play *Justice,* produced in 1910, was the spearhead of these efforts to effect prison reform. 'It has cost me much peace of mind', he wrote, but his efforts were not in vain. The impact of *Justice* helped force through new legislation that significantly reduced solitary confinement in English prisons.

The philanthropist in Galsworthy was now coming into conflict with the artist. The problem was compounded by Ada's increasingly possessive demands on his time and energies, and brought to crisis point by his affair with a young dancer called Margaret Morris. Margaret was 19 and Galsworthy 43 when he invited her to choreograph and appear in his play *The Little Dream.* At first Ada

Thwarted lover
John's first love did not meet with family approval and he was packed off to Russia (above), partly on family business, partly to forget her. For all the scandal of their premarital 'affair', John and Ada's love had little physical expression. In early middle age (left) his love for the young 'expressive' dancer Margaret Morris (right) shook him to the core. They quickly admitted to the affair, and Ada purported to understand his need for sexual fulfilment. But her 'suffering' persuaded John to break with Margaret entirely. After he had done so, Ada ended all sexual relations.

Seeking distractions
To escape the misery of his broken love affair, Galsworthy sailed with Ada to America (above), there to produce his play, The Pigeon, *and to gratify Ada's continual need for diversion. He later assuaged his guilt at not serving in World War I, by training as a masseur and working in France in Bénévole Hospital, to speed the rehabilitation of wounded soldiers (right). Galsworthy is seated, far left.*

was as taken as her husband with the beautiful and talented dancer, and the Galsworthys helped set her up in her own dance school in London. But slowly, in the course of their professional collaboration, and to the great astonishment of both, Galsworthy and Margaret Morris fell in love.

PASSION SUPPRESSED

The final section of his novel *The Dark Flower* recounts with great frankness the history of their doomed passion. Ada put on a brave face when she found out about it, and for a time Galsworthy and Margaret hoped against hope that Ada might agree to share her husband's love. But Galsworthy knew that his love for Margaret could continue only at the expense of Ada's health and happiness.

The affair was effectively ended by his agonized decision to leave the country with Ada. They went first to Paris, then the south of France, then to America, where he was warmly greeted by his reading public. He and Margaret wrote each other frequent letters which showed that their love burned hotter than ever, but Galsworthy's mind was firmly made up – 'You *must* not be unhappy – do you hear, my dear – you must not, because it makes me unhappier', he chided her.

The affair was over, but its repercussions were not so easily dismissed. The trust between Galsworthy and Ada had been shattered and their marriage would continue on much less intimate terms. In rejecting the youthful passion of Mar-

garet Morris he had also chosen to stifle the emotional side of himself, and his writing suffered.

The outbreak of World War I three years later came as a shattering blow to Galsworthy's belief in the essential goodness of humankind. He felt miserably guilty that at the age of 47 he was too old to fight, so for most of the next four years he wrote at a frantic pace and donated the bulk of his earnings to the war effort. He signed over the family house at Cambridge Gate as a rest home for wounded soldiers and at the end of 1916 he and Ada looked after disabled soldiers in a convalescent hospital in France. Still the guilt was not quite exorcized – 'I'm beginning to feel I'm not pulling my weight', he wrote.

In 1917 he turned down the offer of a knighthood from the Prime Minister, Lloyd George – 'I say Literature is its own reward' – though 12 years later he did accept the Order of Merit. He was now a distinguished man of letters, a pillar of the Establishment of which he had once been so critical. With the purchase of Grove Lodge, an impressive house in Hampstead, and, a few years later, Bury House, a 15-bedroom mansion near Pulborough in Sussex, Galsworthy became truly and ironically a man of property like Soames.

In the early post-War years Galsworthy wrote some of his most commercially successful work, including the second and third novels of *The Forsyte Saga* – *In Chancery* and *To Let*. The *Saga* was a bestseller on both sides of the Atlantic.

THE PEN CLUB

The international writers' club PEN was inaugurated on 6 October 1921 by Mrs Dawson Scott, and John Galsworthy was its first president. He was the obvious choice: a campaigner on social and ethical issues, and a respected public figure. After World War I, he was anxious to believe once more in the stated aim of PEN: 'friendship and understanding between writers and . . . freedom of expression within and between all nations.' His presidency lasted ten years and he attended eight International Congresses, though it cost him dear to deliver an address; 'for a shy man to be the focus of a crowd is an ordeal', wrote a fellow member, on seeing him there. At the end of his life, Galsworthy donated his Nobel Prize money – £9,000 – to a PEN trust fund to further the cause to which he so firmly adhered.

Artist's immortality
In his last years, honours were heaped on Galsworthy, the man of letters (left). His ashes were scattered by his nephew on the Sussex Downs (below).

Despite this public acclaim, despite the honorary degrees showered on him from Princeton to Oxford, from Dublin to Cambridge, and the constant requests for lectures and public appearances, Galsworthy was increasingly unhappy with his work, afflicted by a gnawing sense of failure – 'I feel absolutely without hope of ever writing anything worth reading again', he wrote in 1920.

COUNTRY SQUIRE

At Bury House, purchased in 1926, he settled down to the sort of life that, like his fiction, harked back to the pre-War era. 'Now nearly bald with a forehead more terrifically domed than ever', he spent his time horseriding on Bury Hill, playing croquet on the lawn and tennis with house guests. He became a benevolent father figure to the local community, paying small weekly pensions to the poorer families and building cottages for his gardeners and domestic staff.

He was already a dying man when he was awarded literature's highest honour, the Nobel Prize, in 1932. For six months he had lived the life of a recluse, struck dumb by attacks of stuttering, shunning the light after a blemish appeared on his nose, yet stubbornly refusing to see a doctor for fear of alarming Ada. He never delivered the speech he drafted for the Nobel award ceremony in Stockholm – by then he was too ill to travel.

John Galsworthy slipped into a coma on the night of 30 January 1933 and died the following morning at home in Hampstead, from a brain tumour. He was 65. He was cremated and his ashes scattered over Bury Hill.

All her married life, the fragile Ada had expected to die first and to be helped through her last days by John. So distraught and enraged was she at his seeming desertion of her that she burned many of his papers. She could not, however, destroy his lasting fame.

THE FORSYTE SAGA

A richly detailed portrayal of three generations, Galsworthy's masterpiece subtly and ironically reveals the insensitivity and self-seeking passions beneath middle-class respectability.

It was the first volume of *The Forsyte Saga* that brought Galsworthy his breakthrough to success as an author, and although there have been some notable revivals of his plays, his reputation still stands or falls by this famous sequence of novels.

Three books make up *The Forsyte Saga* – *The Man of Property* (1906), *In Chancery* (1920) and *To Let* (1921) – and they were first published together (with two linking 'Interludes') under the collective title in 1922. Galsworthy later wrote two more related trilogies (the nine volumes collectively are called 'The Forsyte Chronicles') and he also used the characters in several short stories, but the *Saga* is complete in itself.

It is easy to understand the lasting popularity of *The Forsyte Saga* and the success with which it was translated to television, for it portrays with an absorbing richness of texture the stratum of society that was the backbone of England's wealth during a Golden Age of prosperity and stability. As young Jolyon says ironically to the architect Bosinney:

"*It's their wealth and security that makes everything possible; makes your art possible, makes literature, science, even religion, possible. Without Forsytes, who believe in none of these things, but turn them all to use, where should we be? My dear sir, the Forsytes are the middlemen, the commercials, the pillars of society, the corner-stones of convention; everything that is admirable!*"

GUIDE TO THE PLOT

The first book of the *Saga* opens in 1886, in the London home of the senior member of the Forsyte family, old Jolyon, at a gathering to celebrate the engagement of his granddaughter, June, to the architect Philip Bosinney. Jolyon, 80 years old but still a vigorous and commanding figure, has made his fortune as a tea merchant. Other members of the family to whom we are introduced are equally pillars of upper-middle-class respectability. Among them is Jolyon's nephew Soames, a solicitor, who is married to the beautiful Irene. Bosinney is from a different world, for he is not only "a young man without fortune", but also dashing, flamboyant and romantic. The family, who nickname him

'The Buccaneer', are rather wary of him, but cannot deny his brains or magnetism.

Missing from the gathering is June's father, Jolyon's son young Jolyon, the 'black sheep' of the family. He has "done for himself by deserting his wife and child and running away with that foreign governess". Young Jolyon, in fact, is now married to the governess, Helène, his first wife having died, and has two young children, Jolly and Holly. Although he has an eminently respectable job as a Lloyd's underwriter, young Jolyon is much less materialistic than other members of the family and devotes much of his time to painting. Old Jolyon surreptitiously buys his pictures from time to

Soulless prosperity (above) The Forsytes live in a world in which financial security, material possessions and adherence to accepted social standards count for everything. "No Forsyte has given a dinner without providing a saddle of mutton"; it has a "succulent solidity . . . like a deposit paid into a bank".

"So you've come back?" (left) When Bosinney is killed, Irene, "not knowing where to turn", goes back to Soames. Her face was "so white and motionless that it seemed as though the blood must have stopped flowing in her veins", and her eyes were "like the great wide, startled brown eyes of an owl".

84

> "... to a true Forsyte, sentiment, even the sentiment of social position, was a luxury only to be indulged in after his appetite for more material pleasure had been satisfied."

time, for after 14 years' estrangement he still cares deeply about his son. One night, feeling "a terrible yearning" to see him, he calls at young Jolyon's club and the two make their peace.

Meanwhile Soames, the 'man of property' of the title, has decided to build a house in the country, Robin Hill, just outside London, and he engages Bosinney as the architect. Soames hopes that the house will bring him closer to Irene, who feels no love for him and regrets the marriage, but instead she and Bosinney fall in love. Infuriated by her indifference to him, Soames decides to exert his rights over his 'property' and rapes Irene.

Bosinney spends more than the agreed limit on the house and Soames successfully sues him. Irene leaves Soames for Bosinney, but Bosinney is knocked down and killed in a road accident. There is talk of suicide, but the general opinion is that, having learned of the rape, "the poor fellow was so cracked with jealousy, so cracked for his vengeance, that he heard nothing of the omnibus in that infernal fog". Irene returns to Soames and young Jolyon goes to offer her his sympathy, but the book ends with Soames slamming the door in his face.

The second part of the trilogy, *In Chancery*, is set about a decade later, and centres on the growing relationship between Irene and young Jolyon. Old Jolyon has died and left Irene a substantial

Street tragedy
Bosinney is killed in a road accident when he is distraught over Soames' attack on Irene.

annuity, of which young Jolyon is the trustee. Young Jolyon's second wife has died, and he now lives with his children at Robin Hill, bought from Soames by old Jolyon. Irene has long since left Soames and lives quietly on her own.

Soames, now in his mid-forties, is desperate to have a son to inherit his

Connoisseur's home
(left) Soames is a knowledgeable collector, but his mind is always on the value of his pictures. June comments that he treats art "as if it were grocery".

Fruitful friendship
(above) Old Jolyon's final years are enriched by friendship with Irene, wife of his nephew Soames. His deep affection for her is reflected in the generous legacy he makes her.

In the Background

BUILDING BOOM

The period covered by *The Forsyte Saga* saw a great increase in London's population and expansion of suburbia. Robin Hill is 12 miles from the centre of town, but Jolyon fears it will be swallowed by "the giant London".

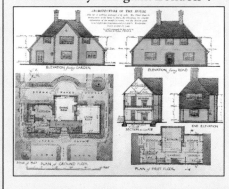

"*His whole life, with every natural instinct and every decent yearning gagged and fettered, and all because Fate had driven him seventeen years ago to set his heart upon this woman . . . Cursed was the day he had met her, and his eyes for seeing in her anything but the cruel Venus she was! And yet . . .*"

Romance in Soho
(below) Obsessed with having an heir, Soames determines to marry Annette, the daughter of a Soho restaurant proprietor. But first he must divorce Irene.

Parisian interlude
(right) Irene hides in Paris from Soames, but he follows her. He thinks she enjoys this "foreign life; she had never been properly English – even to look at!"

---

fortune and is paying court to Annette, a young Frenchwoman who keeps the accounts in her mother's Soho restaurant. Before he can marry her, however, he has to obtain a divorce from Irene. Jolyon goes to see her on his behalf, then Soames himself visits her and finds his old ardour for her rekindled. He attempts to woo her, but Irene is horrified and tells him she would "rather die" than go back to him.

Soames assumes (wrongly) that Irene has a lover, and has her followed by a private detective to try to obtain evidence for a divorce, even when she goes to Paris to escape his attentions. Jolyon, who is falling in love with her, visits Irene in Paris, and Soames in turn goes there to make a last attempt to win her back. His reaction to being thwarted has far-reaching consequences – not just for Irene and Jolyon, Annette and himself, but for the innocent third generation, whose fate is explored in the final volume, set 20 years afterwards.

ELEMENTS OF SATIRE

The Forsyte Saga was favourably reviewed when it first appeared, but generally it has been much more popular with the reading public than with literary critics or fellow-writers. D.H. Lawrence, for example, wrote a well-known critique of Galsworthy in which he said '*The Man of Property* had the elements of a very great novel, a very great satire', but that it 'fizzles out'. Galsworthy, he thought, 'had not quite enough of the superb courage of his satire . . . He might have been the surgeon the modern soul needs so badly, to cut away

the proud flesh of our Forsytes . . . Instead, he put down the knife and laid on a soft, sentimental poultice.'

There is no doubt of the keen satiric intent with which Galsworthy began *The Man of Property* or of the skill with which he carried it off. The opening pages set the tone with an extended description of "that charming and instructive sight – an upper-middle-class family in full plum-age", in which we see how the individual

members of the Forsyte family generally dislike and mistrust each other but are bound together by a sense of solidarity against any threat to the values they cherish so dearly.

Their central value is the importance of property – "The position of their houses was of vital importance to the Forsytes, nor was this remarkable, since the whole spirit of their success was embodied therein." The very personification of

book 'with a purpose', but he was, in the words of his friend Joseph Conrad, 'a humanitarian moralist'. His 'message' is clearly that possessiveness of the Forsyte kind is wrong and degrading. In pursuing his attack, however, Galsworthy faced a dilemma. Although he hated the Forsytes' greed and clannishness, their smugness and contempt for the weak, there was also much in their world that he loved. He was a member of the upper-middle-class himself, and however different he was in outlook from Soames Forsyte, Galsworthy could see things from Soames' point

Charles Leroy-Saint-Aubert: A Young Lady in Paris/Fine Art Photographic Library

Wayward husband
(below) Winifred Forsyte, Soames' sister, marries the rakish, irresponsible Montague Dartie, whose philandering leads to a break-up of their family.

Cousins in love
(right) Romance blossoms after an accidental meeting, but Fleur and Jon Forsyte learn that there is bitter parental opposition to their love.

A. C. Michael: Fleur and Jon. The Bookman Christmas Issue 1928

to see it as a source of strength. If he had continued to satirize Soames as he does in the opening of *The Man of Property*, he might have created a monster or a caricature, but not the thoroughly believable character whose actions we follow through several hundred pages.

LITERARY NOVELTY

Next to Soames the other characters look a little two-dimensional, although Irene is an interesting experiment in presentation. She is deliberately portrayed through other characters' reactions to her, rather than through her own speech and actions. Galsworthy himself wrote: 'she is never present except through the senses of other characters', and the reviewer in *The Scotsman* commented: 'Irene is a remarkable study in impressive silence. She rarely speaks yet both Soames and the reader have an impression conveyed to them that she always has the last word.'

This was Galsworthy's one literary novelty, for he made no pretence at trying to break new ground in technique. Rather, he was proud – and with every justification – of his skills in traditional narrative and construction. *The Forsyte Saga* is a long book with a big cast, but it is put together seamlessly, and the plot and the language flow with a master craftsman's touch. Galsworthy's detractors refer to him disparagingly as a 'middlebrow' writer – someone who writes undemanding books for a mass audience. To his countless admirers, however, he is quite simply one of the best storytellers in the English language.

Charles Hermans: Dawn/Fine Art Photographic Library

Forsyte ideals, and the focus of Galsworthy's attack, is Soames Forsyte, who regards his wife Irene as just as much his property as the house he is building. Unlike other Forsytes, he has an appreciation of beauty, but he collects pictures more because "there was money to be made out of every change of fashion"; and Irene's "power of attraction he regarded as part of her value as his property".

Galsworthy denied that he wrote the

of view as well as from that of the more obviously attractive characters – Irene, young Jolyon and Bosinney.

Galsworthy, in fact, seems to have come not only to sympathize with Soames, but even to identify with him to some extent. Critics who follow D.H. Lawrence's line of thought see this as a source of weakness, preventing Galsworthy from following through his attack on Forsyte values. But it is equally possible

CHARACTERS IN FOCUS

At the beginning of the book Galsworthy describes the Forsytes as a family "no branch of which had a liking for the other, between no three members of whom existed anything worthy of the name of sympathy". The strong antipathies and rivalries, particularly between Soames and young Jolyon, remain throughout the *Saga*, but as Galsworthy warmed to his characters he made his portrayal of them less satirical and more human.

WHO'S WHO

Old Jolyon The Forsyte patriarch, "the figurehead of his family and class and creed . . . the representative of moderation, and order, and love of property".

Young Jolyon Old Jolyon's only child, the family renegade, ruled by his heart rather than head.

Soames Young Jolyon's cousin, a solicitor and picture-collector. He typifies Forsyte values in being "a slave of property".

Irene The beautiful and cultured daughter of a professor, who marries Soames and young Jolyon in turn.

June Young Jolyon's eldest child. She inherits her father's nature.

Philip Bosinney A handsome young architect, "as clever as you like", but "a bit up in the air" by sober Forsyte standards. He is engaged to June, but falls in love with Irene.

Annette A young Frenchwoman who looks after the accounts in her mother's restaurant; she becomes Soames' second wife.

Fleur The daughter of Soames and Annette. Pretty and high-spirited, she is the only woman other than Irene Soames ever loves.

Jon The son of young Jolyon and Irene, "one of those boys (not many) in whom a home-trained love of beauty had survived school".

G. M. Joy. The Bayswater Omnibus (detail). Museum of London/Bridgeman Art Library

"Pale and well-shaved", Soames (left) "conveyed an appearance of reserve and secrecy, of imperturbable, enforced composure"; it is "impossible to conceive of him with a hair out of place, a tie deviating one-eighth of an inch from the perpendicular, a collar unglossed!" He sees everything in materialistic terms and so is unable to understand Irene's rejection of him. But his love for Irene is stronger than any emotion he has ever felt, and it continues to haunt him even in old age, when he has matured into a grumpy but much-respected senior figure.

"A tall woman, with a beautiful figure, which some member of the family had once compared to a heathen goddess", Irene (right) has an overpowering effect on the three men who fall in love with her, and it is mainly through their reactions that she is presented. Bosinney's eyes gaze at her "like a dog's looking at its master", and when Soames goes to see her for the first time in twelve years, he is rendered speechless as his feelings for her come flooding back. Her inscrutable magic works more slowly on Jolyon, but as love flowers between them he asks, "For sheer emotional intensity had he ever – old as he was – passed through such a moment?"

Sir E. J. Poynter: Portrait of a Lady/Fine Art Photographic Library

"Young Jolyon [left] however different he had become in mood and temper, had always retained the neat reticence of Forsyte appearance." "Impressionable and warm-hearted", Jolyon regards himself as "the missing link" between the Forsytes and the world outside the family. "Without me in between", he tells Bosinney, "you would seem like a different species."

"The turn of that creamy neck, her delicate curves . . . What a perfect young thing to hold in one's arms! What a mother for his heir!" So Soames thinks of Annette (right), who gives him the child he wants, but cannot replace Irene.

"His eyes are the truest things I ever saw; and he's quite divinely silent!" says Fleur of her cousin Jon (left), with whom she falls in love. "He's a second cousin – such a child, about six months older and ten years younger than I am." Jon's ardour for Fleur is just as great, but he is put on the rack by his father's pleas to give her up for the sake of his mother's feelings.

The "treasured possession" of Soames' life, Fleur (right) is "frighteningly self-willed, and full of life, and determined to enjoy it". She can soften even her father's expression, and when she hears of the family feud that threatens her relationship with Jon she dismisses it as "ever so romantic and silly", unaware of the bitterness of the feelings involved.

Mansell Collection

Mansell Collection

Arthur Hacker: Young Girl in a Punt. Fine Art Society, London/Bridgeman Art Library

S. P. Kendrick: Reflections/Fine Art Photographic Library

A VOICE FOR FREEDOM

Galsworthy was one of the most successful authors of his time, but he wrote more to express his social conscience than for personal gain. His impact on public opinion was unprecedented.

Although he was eventually to become fluent and prolific, Galsworthy made a slow, unpromising start in literature; it was five years, according to him, before he 'could master even its primary techniques'. The publication of his first book in 1897 gave him a delight that he afterwards recalled with wry amusement: 'my conscience not having yet been born – I was more proud of the vile little body which bound those nine tales under the title *From the Four Winds* than I was of any of its successors.'

Later, when Galsworthy had made his name, he refused to reissue 'that dreadful little book' or the novel that followed it. Altogether, four works under his *nom de plume* 'John Sinjohn' were published before Galsworthy put his own name to a novel – *The Island Pharisees* (1904).

A TRUE PROFESSIONAL

The shaping of that book, and Galsworthy's emergence as a truly professional writer, owed a great deal to the help and advice of Edward Garnett. This extraordinary man – a publisher's reader who himself wrote relatively little – had already 'brought on' Galsworthy's friend

Joseph Conrad, and would in time serve as the mentor of younger writers including D. H. Lawrence and H. E. Bates. Garnett's contacts and expertise helped to place Galsworthy's poems and articles with London newspapers and periodicals; but his chief function was as a rigorous, implacable critic.

The most striking example of Garnett's influence on Galsworthy occurred when he read the manuscript of the first Forsyte novel, *The Man of Property* (1906). At its climax, Bosinney, the architect who is Irene's lover, learns that Soames has raped her; and he is so distraught and despairing that he rushes into the street and flings himself in front of a passing vehicle. Garnett insisted that this suicide was 'an *artistic blot* of a very grave order, psychologically false, and seriously shaking the illusion of the whole story'. After some resistance Galsworthy made a significant concession to Garnett's view, rewriting Bosinney's death in its present, more ambiguous form.

Galsworthy's greatest creation, the Forsyte family, made its first appearance several years before *The Man of Property*. In one of the stories by 'John Sinjohn',

Rural retreat
(right) Galsworthy's remote home in Devon brought back memories of his early life as a gentleman of leisure. In The Country House, *he gently satirized this life, while still being half-attracted to it.*

'The Salvation of Swithin Forsyte', a narrowly prudent, crassly materialistic man becomes dimly aware on his deathbed that his life is unfulfilled. Galsworthy commented that 'I owe Swithin much, for he first released the satirist in me, and is moreover, the only one of my characters whom I killed before I gave him life, for it is in the "Man of Property" [in the form of Soames] that Swithin Forsyte more memorably lives.'

Once embarked on *The Man of Property*, Galsworthy seems to have realized that he had found the perfect subject – the philistine upper-middle-class world from which he himself came. The inhumanity of this world was illuminated by the

The eminent author
At his Sussex mansion, Galsworthy (right) spent his mornings writing, his evenings revising what he had written. His wife, Ada (far right), was his tireless scribe. She not only wrote replies to his voluminous correspondence, but typed up the first three drafts of all his work. That she was a prime source of inspiration to him, as well as a practical help, is shown in the 'super-dedication' he wrote for The Forsyte Saga *(centre right).*

Right: Mansell Collection

By permission of the University of Birmingham

90

Literary friend
Galsworthy valued the encouragement of his friend Joseph Conrad (right), whom he had met on a homebound voyage from Australia. Conrad spotted the potential of Galsworthy's early story 'The Salvation of Swithin Forsyte', but recommended a 'sceptical' detachment. 'There is exquisite atmosphere in your tales. What they want now is more air.'

dramatic suffering endured by his wife during her first marriage, when her husband discovered her illegitimacy. The writing came easily, and during its course Galsworthy's spirits were lifted by the prospect of Ada at last obtaining a divorce and becoming his wife. In his draft acceptance speech for the Nobel Prize, he recalled:

'*The Man of Property* was conceived in satiric mood and carried to its close in a larger spirit; it was written here, there, everywhere, the most scattered of my manuscripts, at the time of my life most poignant. Two-thirds of it had taken nearly two years to write; the last third was written in six weeks, with the pale north-Italian sunlight filtering through winter branches on to the pages. I was, indeed, in no hurry for the appearance of that book; I knew it to be the best I had written; and the revision of it, sentence by sentence, gave me more intimate pleasure than I am likely to have again.'

MARITAL INSPIRATION

Later, when he had expanded this first novel into *The Forsyte Saga*, Galsworthy would dedicate it to Ada, 'without whose encouragement, sympathy, and criticism I could never have become even such a writer as I am.' Ada was indeed the most important single influence on Galsworthy's writing life. Although his friendship with Conrad – the result of a chance meeting on board ship during his travels in 1893 – may have strengthened his desire to write, it seems to have been Ada who provided the decisive impetus. Early in their relationship she must have become aware of his frustrated ambitions, and at Easter 1895, when he was 27 years old, as they parted at the Gare du Nord in

Paris, she is said to have remarked 'Why don't you write? You're just the person.'

Whether or not this was actually the moment at which Galsworthy became a writer, his career began with Ada, and her marital story provided him with his most effective literary subject – one that was not confined to the *Saga*, but was explored again and again in Galsworthy's fiction. During their life together Ada acted as Galsworthy's secretary, indefatigably typing and retyping his drafts, and discussing everything he wrote.

It is possible that in the long run this exclusive devotion was not good for Galsworthy's development as a writer.

Advocate for justice
Galsworthy trained as a barrister, but he disliked the profession intensely. However, he put his legal knowledge to good use, choosing to use his powers of persuasion in the theatre rather than in the Law Courts (left). He did so most successfully in his play Justice, *in which a man is accused of forgery. His defence counsel eloquently argues: 'Justice is a machine that . . . rolls on of itself. Is this young man to be ground to pieces under this machine for an act which at the worst was one of weakness?' The practical result of the play was a reduction in the hours of solitary confinement.*

Constructive critic
The publisher's reader Edward Garnett gave Galsworthy wise counsel when he was working on The Forsyte Saga.

Apart from her ill-health and restless urge to travel – both of which made heavy inroads on Galsworthy's time and attention – Ada's fragile presence was arguably inhibiting, making him unadventurous as both man and writer. There is some evidence that Galsworthy believed this to be so, although he was too much of a gentleman to complain.

RADICAL DRAMA

Typically, his only real outburst on the subject occurred when he was agonizing not over his writing, but over what part he should properly take in the war effort. In his diary he acknowledged that he would not be able to face up to duties that took him away from Ada: 'This is what comes of giving yourself to a woman body and soul. A. paralyses and has always paralysed me.' Galsworthy adds 'I have never been able to face the idea of being cut off from her' – which may have been the simple truth, or a way of taking the blame for the 'paralysis'.

While correcting the proofs of *The Man of Property* during the winter of 1905-6, Galsworthy wrote his first play, *The Silver Box*. He sent it to the management of the Royal Court Theatre, which accepted it immediately – an astonishing piece of good fortune, since it has always been much more difficult to get a play performed than to find a publisher for a novel. As it happened, the Court was committed, at that time, to making radical changes to drama, presenting works by George Bernard Shaw and other writers who were breaking with Victorian conventions and showing the social order in a clear, often unflattering light.

The Silver Box is a tale of twin thefts in which only the man with the money

escapes justice; its lesson is that there is one law for the rich and another for the poor. This was just the sort of play that audiences had been waiting for, and they flocked to see it.

With the concurrent success of *The Man of Property* Galsworthy became celebrated simultaneously as a novelist and playwright. He went on to write over 20 works for the stage, some of which strongly influenced contemporary opinion. His play *Justice* (1910), for example, so moved the Home Secretary, Winston Churchill, that he was persuaded by it that the practice of solitary confinement in prison needed to be reformed.

REDRESSING WRONGS

Galsworthy's plays form a major and seriously underrated part of his literary output; as a number of television productions have shown, their human and dramatic qualities have enabled them to survive the social problems they deal with. That is not to say, however, that the issues have always become dated over the years – the theme of the labour dispute in *Strife* (1909), for example, is as relevant today as it was almost 80 years ago.

In his plays, and in his many essays and articles, Galsworthy takes a strong reforming stance, attacking specific legal abuses and social injustices. By contrast, as a novelist he is primarily a satirist of the upper and upper-middle class. In the years following *The Man of Property* he tackled the English squirearchy in *The Country House* (1907); wealthy philanthropists – very much like himself – in *Fraternity* (1909); and political life in *The Patrician* (1911). It was only in 1917, to escape the stress of war (which the idealistic Galsworthy ruefully called 'the grand defeat of all Utopians'), that he returned to his most successfully executed subject with a story, *Indian Summer of a Forsyte*.

CONTINUING THE *SAGA*

A year later, he realized the full potential of the Forsytes. 'I think the July Sunday at Wingstone in 1918, when it suddenly came to me that I could go on with my Forsytes, and complete their history in two more volumes with a link between, was the happiest day of my writing life.'

Many characters in the *Saga* originated as portraits of the Galsworthy family (old Jolyon, for example, was based on Galsworthy's own father), and Galsworthy's sister was so alarmed that she urged him to delay publication of *The Man of Property* for a few years. Galsworthy was unrepentant: 'The artist can as a rule only

Triumphant sequel
A Modern Comedy *clinched Galsworthy's success, as the above promotional display suggests.*

'Strife'
(right) This political play added to Galsworthy's fame as a dramatist.

City attractions
(left) *Although a lover of country life, Galsworthy could not manage without the social stimulus of the town, both as a man and as a writer. Paradoxically, he needed contact with the moneyed classes he mocked in his novels; and he obviously benefited from meetings with fellow-writers. But he liked to live out of 'the thick of things', as he put it, and made Grove Lodge in Hampstead (right) his London home. Here he spent his mornings working undisturbed at the top of the house, after an early invigorating ride on Hampstead Heath.*

reproduce that, or things similar to that, which he has felt.' But he also insisted that characters altered and developed in the course of writing, so that a fictional individual 'at every sentence diverges more and more from the original'. This was true above all of Soames, who begins as a brute (based on Ada's ex-husband) and eventually becomes the real hero of the *Saga*. Furthermore, the Forsytes and

their world – originally a target for Galsworthy's satire – are shown in an increasingly attractive light under the joint impulses of post-War nostalgia and fictional logic.

Galsworthy's later novels show a progressive loss of power, although he completed two more trilogies, *A Modern Comedy* (1924–8), about the Forsytes, and the closely related *End of the Chapter* (1931–3), as well as a book of short stories, *On Forsyte 'Change* (1930).

PASSPORT TO PERMANENCE

Ironically, it was during this period of decline that he became a best-selling author in Britain and the United States, when sales of his works ran into millions. The negative reaction, when it came, was equally extreme, and Galsworthy's novels were largely neglected until the revival of the 1960s. Then the television version of *The Forsyte Saga* (first broadcast in 1967) demonstrated that the book's qualities of narrative and characterization had stood the test of time. As Galsworthy himself prophesied, '*The Forsyte Saga* . . . will be my passport, however heavily visaed, for the shores of permanence.'

After an unpromising start with short stories and mediocre novels, Galsworthy found his voice as a social satirist with *The Island Pharisees* (1904). Published under his own name, it was the first book which gave him the confidence to abandon his alias. *The Man of Property* (1906) was an instant popular and critical success and Galsworthy became equally celebrated as a playwright with *The Silver Box* (1906), *Strife* (1909) and *Justice* (1910), all of which tackled moral and social issues. After an interval of fourteen years he returned to the Forsytes, completing the *Saga* in 1921-22 and simultaneously scoring another dramatic triumph with *Loyalties* (1922). The main Forsyte narrative – and the life of the central character, Soames – comes to an end in a further trilogy entitled *A Modern Comedy* (1924-28). The television dramatization of the *Saga* 40 years later attested to the timelessness of Galsworthy's writing.

E. van Gelder: La Grande Place/Fine Art Photographic Library

A MODERN COMEDY
◆ 1929 ◆

Unfulfilled in her marriage, Fleur Mont (right) falls briefly in love with a poet, Wilfred Desert, in *The White Monkey*, the first book in this second Forsyte trilogy, which takes up the story where the *Saga* left it. Fleur's publisher husband, Michael Mont, has been forced to fire an employee, Tony Bicket, and Bicket's ensuing poverty has led his desperate wife, Victorine, to pose as an artist's model (far right). When Michael Mont goes into politics in *The Silver Spoon*, Fleur's social ambitions involve her in a damaging court case. The man she has always loved, Jon Forsyte, returns to England with his wife in the final novel, *Swan Song*. Fleur tries desperately to win him back, but Jon, though strongly tempted, resists her. The distraught Fleur accidentally causes a fire at her father's house, and for Soames the conflict between Property and Beauty is at last resolved.

THE ISLAND PHARISEES
◆ 1904 ◆

A starving Frenchman, Louis Ferrand (left), speaks for 'the rebellious underside of life' in this scathing dissection of British society. The main character, Richard Shelton, is a wealthy, idealistic young man who abandons his profession as a barrister, but cannot fix on some more worthwhile pursuit. For a time love fills up his life, and he becomes engaged to the attractive, apparently sensitive Antonia Dennant. But visits to Britain's slums and prisons open Shelton's eyes to social injustice, as does his friendship with the destitute Ferrand. While Shelton comes to see the entire social system in terms of well-fed hypocrisy, Antonia is simply puzzled and alarmed by his views, and their relationship reaches a crisis.

U. Ricant: The Tryst/Fine Art Photographic Library

London Library

The Bookman Christmas Issue 1928

JUSTICE
→1910←

The English legal system (above) is the subject of this ironically titled play. William Falder, a young lawyer's clerk, forges a cheque in order to help the woman he loves to escape from her cruel and selfish husband. For this one foolhardy act Falder has to serve three long years in prison, much of the time in solitary confinement. While 'justice' is served in the legal sense, Galsworthy shows that it is in no way served morally. The very harsh sentence is disproportionate to the crime and the aftermath for Falder is devastating. On the first night of the play's performance, the gallery audience were so moved that they stayed in the theatre, cheering and refusing to leave until nearly midnight, in the hope of seeing Galsworthy take a bow.

LOYALTIES
→1922←

Ferdinand De Levis (above) has a large sum of money stolen from his room in this play. He becomes convinced that a party guest, Ronald Dancy, is the thief, but De Levis is a Jew and none too popular, whereas Dancy has been a brilliant officer in the War – and 'belongs'. The ranks close against De Levis and, threatened with ostracism, he agrees to remain silent. Notwithstanding this, he is blackballed for membership of a club. Then he repeats his accusation, and a suspiciously reluctant Dancy is forced to sue him for slander. Initially, one kind of loyalty is responsible for vital evidence being withheld, but when the missing banknotes turn up, a different set of loyalties comes into play.

G. S. Watson: Marishka. Private Collection/Bridgeman Art Library

**Edwardian theatre was slow to rise to the challenge of social comment.
Then came a new breed of playwrights who drew audiences
with realistic controversial drama concerning ordinary people.**

In 1906 Galsworthy completed his first play, *The Silver Box.* His friend and mentor, Edward Garnett, immediately recommended it for the Royal Court Theatre in Chelsea. There, J. E. Vedrenne and Harley Granville-Barker were achieving the impossible – attracting large and fashionable audiences to new, daring, experimental plays of the kind formerly confined to small, amateur productions. Granville-Barker was one of the angry young men of the Edwardian theatre,

Prophet of gloom
Henrik Ibsen (right) has been called 'the father of modern drama' because he was first to use the stage to debate contemporary social dilemmas, as in his best known play, about a claustrophobic marriage, A Doll's House *(below).*

and his work at the Royal Court challenged the Establishment with the new 'Theatre of Ideas', or 'Theatre of the Real'.

During Victoria's reign, the stage was dominated by actor-managers who directed their own companies and usually played the leading parts themselves. The emphasis was on entertainment – this was the heyday of the music hall and burlesque. And even in 'legitimate' theatre the style of acting was mannered and highly artificial. Writers were expected to deliver a regular ration of 'fat' parts and star moments per play, each act ending with a suitably momentous curtain-line and tableau. The more special effects and clichés the better, and any dramatic meaning was drowned out in greasepaint.

There had been no attempt to tackle topical, contentious subjects – no references to the impact of Darwinism, to the struggles of the new trades unions, or to the emerging women's emancipation movement. The serious, even sensational issues

Fringe to mainstream
Ibsenites – young, enthusiastic intellectuals inspired by Ibsen – seized on the idea of theatre as a political force. But it took a generation of playwrights remarkable for its flair, daring and talent to bring this kind of play from private performance to public platform. A trip to the theatre (above) became both a social event and stimulating opportunity for education and contentious debate.

Diet of froth
Up until the turn of the century, the theatre-going public were accustomed to a diet of light, undemanding entertainment – music hall, burlesque (left), smoking concerts, operettas, melodramas and sitting-room comedies. There was a clear class division between the bawdy, raucous night out for the working classes and the elegant social occasion enjoyed by the furred and bejewelled wealthy. Shakespearian works were the only survivors from a more edifying age, and they were frequently edited and 'improved upon' and made a vehicle for star names mounting 'virtuoso' performances.

addressed in contemporary novels (including Galsworthy's) were simply not the stuff of Victorian theatre, which fed the public on a diet of melodrama and drawing-room, 'cup-and-saucer' comedies.

Harley Granville-Barker was an actor-manager, but one cast in a new mould. He had a very different approach to the plays he directed at the Royal Court. His actors had to unlearn all the florid mannerisms and learn a new, naturalistic technique, with subtlety of movement, facial expression and gesture. The plays had to work without virtuoso set-pieces and, most important, had to have a social message.

Two towering figures dominated the Theatre of Ideas. Their technique for stirring the social conscience could hardly have been more different – one harrowing the very souls of his audiences with bleak, remorseless tragedies, the other more often impaling his audience on shafts of wit and making them laugh their own and society's folly to scorn.

Henrik Ibsen, the great Norwegian playwright, died in the very year of Galsworthy's theatre debut. Ibsen's plays were gloomy masterpieces offering 'Lessons' on the hypocrisy and dual standards of society. He took for his subjects, for example, the role of women in society and the consequences of inherited syphilis. When Ibsen's *A Doll's House* was first performed in London in 1889 it triggered a major debate on the inadequacies of the commerical theatre. 'Ibsenites' – young enthusiasts for the new plays – got together in clubs called Saturday Night Societies to perform works by their hero.

THEATRICAL COLOSSUS

George Bernard Shaw, a fervent apostle of Ibsen's, grew to be the true colossus of the new theatre. By the time of his death, at the age of 94 in 1950, this Irish writer was one of the most famous men in Britain. He began his literary career as a novelist, without success. But he also worked as a critic of music and drama. In fact, he wrote his first play in collaboration with William Archer,

Granville-Barker
His prodigious talent made him a male lead at 20, a theatre manager before he was 30. He made the Royal Court a rostrum from which a new breed of actor expressed new ideas.

By permission of the University of Birmingham

foremost critic of the exaggerated actor-manager style of drama. Archer was responsible for translating Ibsen into English, and it was he who made Shaw an Ibsenite.

Shaw was a highly political animal. He was a leading Fabian socialist who delighted in controversy. He almost teased the media with paradoxical, deliberately shocking comments on matters of public interest. Even without his literary statements, Shaw would have been famous as a personality – everyone knew of the Jaeger suits he wore as an exponent of the 'rational dress movement', and of his vegetarianism. The word 'Shavian' entered the language as an adjective describing ironic wit. But at first, his plays were simply not staged.

THE SILVER BOX

In the 1890s, Shaw earned more money from the foreign rights of his plays than he had from productions in England. Denied the proper outlet for his plays, he published two volumes of them in 1898 under the title *Plays Pleasant and Unpleasant*, including unusually full stage directions, so that the reader could imagine an ideal production. Shaw revelled in dramas dealing with such issues as slum landlordism, prostitution and the archaic marriage laws which enslaved women. In the preface to *Plays Unpleasant* he wrote: 'I must . . . warn my readers that my attacks are directed against themselves, not against my stage figures.'

Granville-Barker established Shaw as a performed playwright in Britain by staging his plays at the Royal Court. In his early twenties he had already played the lead in several of Shaw's plays, and he was still in his twenties when he staged Galsworthy's *The Silver Box*. Galsworthy approved of Shaw, and Shaw approved of *The Silver Box*, but the two men were very different writers and individuals.

98

Courting success
Harley Granville-Barker, George Bernard Shaw and Galsworthy were united by their work for the Royal Court. They are seen above (left to right) at Galsworthy's farmhouse.

George Bernard Shaw
A shy, eccentric mystic, Shaw (below) ironically cut a flamboyant, provocative figure, with notoriously progressive views. His plays are witty and thought-provoking.

Mary Evans Picture Library

Although not funny, like Shaw's *Pygmalion*, or witty like *Man and Superman*, it is easy to see why *The Silver Box* found favour with the Theatre of Ideas, and why it was accepted by the Royal Court. The valuable box in question belongs in the home of a wealthy Liberal Member of Parliament to which the dissolute young son of the family returns drunk after an evening spent with a prostitute. With him, equally drunk, is Jones, the out-of-work husband of the household's cleaning lady. The embittered Jones, in a spontaneous act of resentment at young Jack Barthwick's opulent lifestyle, removes the silver box. The charwoman is the first to be suspected of theft, and when the box is duly found in Jones' tenement room, the couple are arrested for theft. But it soon becomes clear to the senior Barthwick, the MP, that the legal proceedings may expose his son's scandalous behaviour.

In the last Act, set in a London police court, money, connections and privilege are used to put Jones in prison and muzzle the Press. As Barthwick junior swaggers away, Mrs Jones, who has been left to look after her children alone, appeals to his father's conscience, and is shaken off.

The play's point is that there is one law for the rich and one for the poor. The dissolute Barthwick has absolutely no redeeming qualities. But the most disturbing thing for the Edwardian audience was the depressing, unresolved ending. As one critic wrote, *The Silver Box* was not a cheerful play, 'but if you neglect to see it you will probably miss seeing a play which will continually be quoted when the new school of dramatists has been established.' New repertory companies who were introducing the Theatre of Ideas to other

Mansell Collection

British cities immediately included Galsworthy's dramas in their repertoires. The Liverpool Rep. began life with a production of *Strife*, Galsworthy's play about industrial relations.

A major obstacle stood in the way of this new school of dramatists: censorship by the Lord Chamberlain. It was an obstacle which had never hampered the old-style plays, simply because there was rarely any strong meat in them. Shaw's 'unpleasant play', *Mrs Warren's Profession*, on the other hand, revolves around the discovery by a respectable young heiress that her mother is a former prostitute whose fortune derives from brothels. It was written and published in the 1890s, but because of censorship could not be professionally produced until 1925.

Then Edward Garnett's play *The Breaking Point* suffered mutilation at the hands of the Lord Chamberlain's officials, in the summer of 1907. A few months later, Granville-Barker's play *Waste* was censored. Their mutual friend Galsworthy was roused to action.

WRITERS AGAINST CENSORSHIP

His status as a leading man of letters meant that he was better placed than many of his fellow dramatists to launch a campaign against insensitive and arbitrary censorship. The first concerted protest took the form of a letter signed by three leading writers of the day: Galsworthy, Gilbert Murray and J. M. Barrie. It was sent to every writer of standing in the country, to elicit their support for a change in the law. When 71 writers had cooperated, the Prime Minister was obliged to take notice – or at least to make a show of doing so. An anti-censorship deputation was received at Down-

W. P. Frith: Retribution. By permission of Birmingham Museum and Art Gallery

ing Street. Optimistically, the writers set about drafting a Parliamentary Bill to reform the mechanism of censorship and to allow some means of appeal. Galsworthy contributed to this campaign a powerfully written pamphlet sarcastically entitled *A Justification of the Censorship of Plays*. When a Parliamentary Committee was set up to investigate the whole question, Galsworthy was a star witness. After elaborate deliberations, this Parliamentary Committee produced a report . . . which had no practical effect whatsoever.

In the long run, the censors' teeth were drawn by time rather than protest. After conventional 'Victorian' society had been shattered by World War I, the arrogant liberties taken by Edwardian Lords Chamberlain became unthinkable.

But, for Galsworthy, the whole protest had been a weary, demoralizing experience. Years later, in 1931, when his support was sought for

Prisoners' plea
Galsworthy campaigned for improved conditions for prisoners (above). Though political agitation achieved little, his 1910 play Justice *had such impact that legislation followed as a direct result. In the play, a fundamentally good man is destroyed pointlessly and unthinkingly by the legal system and by those who enforce it. Routine solitary confinement was the prime target for Galsworthy's scathing attack.*

Contrasting styles
Galsworthy's first play,
The Silver Box *(left), is a serious and sober examination of how the law serves the purposes of the rich and crushes the poor beneath its remorseless wheels.*
Shaw's 1912 play
Androcles and the Lion *(right) claims that in order for life to be worth living, it must contain something worth dying for.*
Ultimately, Shaw's wit and lightness of touch gave a longer lasting appeal to his plays than the earnestness of other writers, though Galworthy's do warrant revival.

BBC Hulton Picture Library

another campaign against censorship, he replied, 'I have become reconciled to the evil as the least violent form of interference. Therefore if my opinion must be given, I should say leave the matter alone. For nothing anyway will come of a protest.' It was a sad admission of defeat.

Outside the theatre, the pleas of the new play-wrights carried little weight. But inside the theatre, as Galsworthy proved himself, it was a different story. He was a great campaigner for prison reform – particularly in the matter of solitary confinement. This was a fact of life for all prisoners at the time. It was imposed for three months on first-time offenders and nine months of the year on habitual offenders. On his repeated visits to prison, particularly Dartmoor and Lewes, Galsworthy saw for himself the pointless and physically devastating effect of this form of punishment. What was the object of driving criminals mad? It was as inhumane as it was counter-productive.

Galsworthy tackled the problem in his most powerful play, *Justice,* a searing account of how one ordinary criminal, a man called Falder, who is guilty of altering a cheque, endures solitary confinement.

CAMPAIGNING FOR JUSTICE

While he wrote, Galsworthy campaigned, too. He used his status to get into the prisons and talk to prisoners. He wrote letters to the Press and initiated a public debate. He lobbied important officials of the prison service as well as leading politicians. With all this activity, he was uninten-tionally building up the pre-publicity for the play (directed by Granville-Barker in 1910). After enduring the agony of Falder (who commits his

New ideas

One well-known survivor of the Theatre of Ideas is Shaw's Pygmalion; *in the 1920s, the celebrated actress Mrs Patrick Campbell made the part of Eliza Doolittle her own (above). Modern audiences, however, have preferred to see didactic drama watered down with glamour and frivolity and to watch* Pygmalion *in the gilded disguise of* My Fair Lady. *As early as the 1930s, a newer, brighter theatre swept aside the Theatre of Ideas, which some critics thought worthy but slow-moving. Bertolt Brecht's* The Threepenny Opera *(above right) was as intellectually stimulating as Galsworthy or Shaw, but it was also extremely colourful, incorporating lively songs. It completely rejected the idea that drama should mirror reality, and Brecht's stylized approach had an enormous influence on the up-and-coming generation of young dramatists.*

crime to help a woman being brutalized by her husband), the audience was stunned. The whole issue of solitary confinement was on the agenda for reform. *Justice*'s impact can be compared with that of *Uncle Tom's Cabin,* which roused popular feeling in the United States against slavery.

During his campaign, the Home Secretary, Herbert Gladstone, had told Galsworthy that solitary confinement would be reduced to three months for all offenders. After the play, the new Home Secretary, Winston Churchill, told Gals-worthy that further reductions were being put into effect.

Gilbert Murray was quick and generous with praise. 'It is a fine thing to have achieved, a really great thing. Does not real life seem a tremendous thing as compared with art when one gets the two together? I mean, how much greater it is to have saved a lot of men and women from two months' solitary confinement than to have sent any num-ber of over-fed audiences into raptures.'

For all Murray's kindly meant sentiments, Galsworthy wanted to be both a great playwright and a successful reformer. When asked whether he would prefer *Justice* to become a theatrical classic without any practical results, or to be forgotten as a play but achieve great reforms, the honest artist in him had to opt for enduring fame.

By the late 1920s, Galsworthy's plays had become perfectly acceptable for commercial theatres in the West End. Avant-garde drama was in the hands of Expressionists, Nihilists, the cult of the Absurd . . . Ironically, its actors had reverted to unrealistic dialogue and stylized tech-niqes. These new modernists were scornful of the stale, merely 'photographic' Theatre of the Real, forgetting what priceless ground it had won.

BIBLIOGRAPHY

Abraham, Richard, *Alexander Kerensky: The First Love of the Revolution.* Columbia University Press (New York, 1987)

Aiyer, R. Sadasiva, *Introduction to Galsworthy's Plays.* Folcroft (Folcroft, 1925)

Alkon, Paul K., *Origins of Futuristic Fiction.* University of Georgia Press (Athens, 1987)

Allen, Elizabeth, *A Woman's Place in the Novels of Henry James.* St Martin's Press (New York, 1984)

Appignanesi, Richard, *Lenin for Beginners.* Pantheon Books (New York, 1979)

Batchelor, John, *H. G. Wells.* Cambridge University Press (New York, 1985)

Boyd, Ernest, *Guy de Maupassant: A Biographical Study* (reprint of 1926 edition). Richard West (Philadelphia, 1973)

Britain, Ian, *Fabianism and Culture: A Study in British Socialism and the Arts, c. 1884-1918.* Cambridge University Press (New York, 1982)

Buck, Stratton, *Gustave Flaubert.* G. K. Hall (Boston, 1966)

Burt, Forrest D., *W. Somerset Maugham.* G. K. Hall (Boston, 1985)

Costa, Richard H., *H. G. Wells.* G. K. Hall (Boston, 1985)

Edel, Leon, *Henry James: A Life.* Harper & Row (New York, 1985)

Franc, Miriam A., *Ibsen in England.* Folcroft (Folcroft, 1919)

Gindin, James, *John Galsworthy's Life and Art: An Alien's Fortress.* University of Michigan Press (Ann Arbor, 1987)

Glendinning, Victoria, *Rebecca West.* Alfred A. Knopf (New York, 1987)

Guyot, Edouard, *John Galsworthy* (reprint of 1932 edition). Arden Library (Darby, 1978)

Hart-Davis, Rupert, *Hugh Walpole.* David & Charles (North Pomfret, 1985)

Haynes, R. D., *H. G. Wells: Discoverer of the Future: The Influence of Science on His Thought.* New York University Press (New York, 1980)

Henderson, Archibald, *Bernard Shaw, Playboy and Prophet* (reprint of 1932 edition). Arden Library (Darby, 1985)

Hills, Patricia, *John Singer Sargent.* Harry N. Abrams (New York, 1986)

Huang, John, *Shaw and Galsworthy.* Folcroft (Folcroft, 1932)

Huxley, Leonard, *The Life and Letters of Thomas Henry Huxley* (reprint of 1901 edition). Richard West (Philadelphia, 1979)

Jefferson, George, *Edward Garnett: A Life in Literature.* State Mutual Book (New York, 1981)

Jensen, Sven A., *William Somerset Maugham: Some Aspects of the Man and His Work.* Folcroft (Folcroft, 1957)

Jones, Vivien, *James the Critic.* St Martin's Press (New York, 1985)

Kennedy, Dennis, *Granville Barker and the Dream of Theatre.* Cambridge University Press (New York, 1985)

Marrot, Harold V., *The Life and Letters of John Galsworthy* (reprint of 1936 edition). Augustus M. Kelley (New York, 1973)

Maugham, Robin, *Somerset and All the Maughams* (reprint of 1966 edition). Greenwood Press (Westport, 1977)

Meisel, Martin, *Shaw and the Nineteenth Century Theater.* Limelight Editions (New York, 1984)

Nettels, Elsa, *James and Conrad.* University of Georgia Press (Athens, 1977)

Raphael, Federick, *W. Somerset Maugham and His World.* Scribner's (New York, 1977)

Reed, John R., *The Natural History of H. G. Wells.* Ohio University Press (Athens, 1982)

Rothschild, Loren R., ed., *The Letters of William Somerset Maugham to Lady Juliet Duff.* Rasselas Press (Pacific Palisades, 1982)

Sicker, Philip, *Love and the Quest for Identity in the Fiction of Henry James.* Princeton University Press (Princeton, 1980)

Smith, David, *H. G. Wells: Desperately Mortal.* Yale University Press (New Haven, 1986)

Sternlicht, Sanford, *John Galsworthy.* G. K. Hall (Boston, 1987)

Tanner, Tony, *Henry James: The Writer and His Work.* University of Massachusetts Press (Amherst, 1985)

Thomas, David, *Henrik Ibsen.* Grove Press (New York, 1984)

Thomson, Belinda, *Gauguin.* Thames & Hudson (New York, 1987)

Towne, Charles H., *W. Somerset Maugham, Novelist, Essayist, Dramatist* (reprint of 1925 edition). Folcroft (Folcroft, 1976)

West, Nigel, *MI5: British Security Service Operations, 1909-1945.* Stein & Day (Briarcliff Manor, 1982)

INDEX

Note Page numbers in italic type refer to illustrations.

A

Abbey, Ned 27
Aldiss, Brian 52
Amazing Stories 42, 52
Ambassadors, The (James) 10, 20, 21, *21,* 24
American, The (James) 7, 8
Andersen, Hendrik 9
Anderson, Mary 27
Androcles and the Lion (Shaw) *99*
Ann Veronica (Wells) 33, 43, 45, 47, *47*
'Annette' of *The Forsyte Saga* 86, *86,* 88, *89*
Anticipations (Wells) 42
'Archer, Isabel' of *The Portrait of a Lady* 9, 12, *12,* 13, *13,* 14, *14,* 15, *15,* 16, 17, *17*
Archer, William 97
Ashenden (Maugham) 69, 70, *70, 75,* 76
Aspern Papers, The (James) 19, 21, 23, *23*
Asquith, Herbert 11
Atlee, Clement 35

B

Barrie, J. M. 6, 99
Bates, H. E. 90
Battle of Dorking, The (Chesney) *39*
Beaverbrook, Lord 58
Beerbohm, Max *11, 32*
Bell, Clive 56
Belloc, Hilaire *43*
Bennett, Arnold 10, 56, 58
Benson, A. C. 20
Bishop's Apron, The (Maugham) 56
Bosanquet, Theodora 20, *20*
'Bosinney, Philip' of *The Forsyte Saga* 80, 84, *84,* 85, *85,* 87, 88, *88,* 89, 90
Bostonians, The (James) 8, 20, 21, 23, *23*
Brave New World (Huxley) 52
Brecht, Bertolt *100*
Buellens, Abbe 74
Burne Jones, Edward 27
Burroughs, Edgar Rice 52, *52*
Butler, Samuel 48

C

Cakes and Ale (Maugham) 59, *67,* 68, 69, 71, *71*
Cameron, Cecil 73
Campbell, Mrs Patrick *100*
Cantos (Pound) 28
'Carey, Philip' of *Of Human Bondage* 55, 58, 60, *60-61,* 62, *62,* 63, *63,* 64, *65,* 68
Carr, Sybil 79
Cavell, Edith 73, *73*
Chesney, Sir George *39*
Chesterton, G. K. *43*
Christmas Holiday (Maugham) 67
Churchill, Winston 58, 92, 100
Circle, The (Maugham) 58, 66
Conrad, Joseph 9, *11,* 32, 39, 42, 87, 90, 91, *91*
Cooper, Constance Fenimore 8, 9
Country House, The (Galsworthy) *90,* 92
Coward, Noel 58
Crane, Stephen 9, *11,* 27-28
'Cronshaw' of *Of Human Bondage* 62, 63, 64, *65*
'Curate' of *The War of the Worlds* 38, 39, *39,* 40, *41*
Cyrano de Bergerac *48,* 49, 50

D

Dark Flower, The (Galsworthy) 82
Dartie, Montague 87
Davis, Bette *61, 68*
Defoe, Daniel 490
Dickens, Charles 18, 43, 49
Doll's House, A (Ibsen) *96,* 97
Don Fernando (Maugham) 67
Doubleday, Nelson 59

E

East of Suez (Maugham) 58
Edel, Leon 6
Eliot, George 6
Eliot, T. S. 28, *28*
End of the Chapter (Galsworthy) 93
Erewhon (Butler) 48
Ernst, Karl 73
espionage, World War I 72-76, *72-76*

Essay in Autobiography (Wells) 42
Eugenie Granet (Balzac) 19
Europeans, The (James) 19, 21, *21*
expatriates, American, in Europe 24-28, *24-28*

F

Feuchtwanger, Lion 59
First Men in the Moon, The (Wells) 50
Flaubert, Gustave 6, 7, *7, 9*
Ford, Ford Maddox 9, 32
Forster, E. M. 40
Forsyte Saga, The (Galsworthy) 78, 80, 82, 84-89, *84-89,* 90, *90,* 91, 92, *92,* 93, 94
'Forsyte family,' members of, of *The Forsyte Saga* 78, 80, 82, 84-90, *84-89,* 92, 93, 94
Four Quartets, The (Eliot) *28*
Fraternity (Galsworthy) 92
From the Earth to the Moon (Verne) 50
From the Four Winds (Galsworthy) 90

G

Galsworthy, Ada 70, 80, *80,* 81, *81,* 82, *82,* 83, 90, 91, 92
Galsworthy, Arthur 79, 80
Galsworthy, Blanche 78, *78*
Galsworthy, John 77, *77, 90*
  affair with Margaret Morris 81, *81,* 82
  as barrister 70, *91*
  as president of PEN 83, *83*
  as social reformer 81, 92, 99, *99,* 100
  birth 78
  career 90-93, *90-93*
  D. H. Lawrence's views on 86
  death 83
  honours 82, 83
  key dates 78
  marriage 80
  Nobel Prize 83, 91
  nom de plume 90
  school 78-79, *79*
  'Theatre of Ideas' and 96, 97, 98, *98,* 99, *99,* 100
  university 79, *80*

views on *The Forsyte Saga* 93
World War I and 82, *82,* 83, 92
writing apprenticeship 80
Galsworthy, John, senior 78, *78,* 79, 80, 92
Galsworthy, Mabel 80
Garbo, Greta 70, *70*
Garnett, Edward 80, 90, *92,* 96, 99
Gauguin, Paul 57, 69, *69*
Gentleman in the Parlour, The (Maugham) 67
Gernsback, Hugo 52
Gissing, George 32
Gladstone, Herbert 100
Golden Bowl, The (James) 10, 19, 20, 21, 22, *22*
'Goodwood, Caspar' of *The Portrait of a Lady* 12, 16 *16-17*
Gosse, Edmund *11*
Granville-Barker, Harley 96, 97, *97,* 98, *98,* 99, 100
Greaves, Walter 25
Gulliver's Travels (Swift) 48, *49*
Guy Domville (James) 9, 10

HI

Harvey, Laurence *68*
Haxton, Gerald 57, *57,* 58, *58,* 59
Heart of Darkness (Conrad) 39
Herschel, Sir John 50
Hersey, Harold 52
History of Mr Polly, The (Wells) 33, 43, 45, 47, *47*
Home and Beauty (Maugham) 58
Hunt, Holman 18
Huxley, Aldous 52
Huxley, T. H. *30,* 31
I Spied for France (Richard) 74
Ibsen, Henrik *96,* 97, 98
Icaromenippus (Lucian) 49
In Chancery (Galsworthy) 82, 84, 85
In the Days of the Comet (Wells) 42-43
Indian Summer of a Forsyte (Galsworthy) 92
Inferno (Dante) 49
Invisible Man, The (Wells) 31, 42, 45, 46, *46,* 51, *51,* 52
Island of Dr Moreau, The (Wells) 31, 36, 42, 45, *45*
Island Pharisees, The (Galsworthy) 90, 94, *94*

J

James, Alice 7, 8, 9
James, Henry 5, *5, 6*, 12, *18*
  Beerbohm drawing of *11*
  birth 6
  burials 11
  burning of letters/notebooks
    10
  career 18-20, *18-20*
  characters 16-17, *16-17*
  childhood 6
  Constance Fenimore Cooper
    and 8, 9
  death 11
  first night of *Guy Domville*
    and 10
  H. G. Wells and 32, 44
  honorary degree from
    Harvard *11*
  imagery 15
  intimate relationships 9-10
  John Singer Sargent and 25
  key dates 7
  literary debut 6, *8*
  Mark Twain and 25
  medical treatment at
    Malvern *9*
  mother's death and 8
  nervous breakdown 10
  notebook sketches *9*
  Order of Merit 11
  preface to *The Portrait of a
    Lady* 14
  serialized fiction 19
  70th birthday 10
  Stephen Crane and 28
  strokes 11
  views on American tourists
    24
  views on art 18
  views on Civil War 7
  views on English-American
    world 28
  views on Millet 27
  working methods 19-20
  works in outline 21-23,
    21-23
James, Henry, senior 6, *6*, 8
James, Mary 6, *6*, 8
James, Robertson 7, 10
James, Wilky 7, 8
James, William 6, 10, *11*
Justice (Galsworthy) 81, *91*, 92,
  94, 95, *95*, *99*, 100
*Justification of the Censorship of
  Plays, A* (Galsworthy) 99

K

Kelly, Gerald 56
Kemble, Fanny 19
Kerensky, Alexander 58, 75,
  75, 76
Kipling, Rudyard *11*, 39, 59, 67

Kipps (Wells) 43, 45, 46, *46*
Kirke, Walter 73
Kropotkin, Sasha *75*

L

Lady Frederick (Maugham) 56
Lamb House 9, *10-11, 18,* 20,
  20
Lawrence, D. H. 58, 86, 87, 90
Le Carré, John 76
Leacock, Stephen 52
Lenin, V. I. 34, *34,* 75, 76, *76*
Leyland, Frederick 26
Little Dream, The (Galsworthy)
  81
Liza of Lambeth (Maugham)
  56, 66, *66-67,* 69, *69*
Lloyd George, David 82
Lost World (Doyle) 49
'Louisa, Aunt' of *Of Human
  Bondage* 60, 61, 62, 64, *65*
Love and Mr Lewisham (Wells)
  43, *43*
Loyalties (Galsworthy) 94, 95,
  95

M

Mackenzie, Sir Compton 20,
  72, 73, 76
Man and Superman (Shaw) 98
Man of Honour, A
  (Maugham) 56
Man of Property, The
  (Galsworthy) 80, 84, 86,
  87, 90, 91, 92, 94
Man Who Would Be King, The
  (Kipling) 39
'Martians' of *The War of the
  Worlds* 37, *37,* 38, *38-39,*
  39, 40, *40-41,* 41
Mason, A. E. W. 76
Mata Hari 74, *74*
Maugham, Edith Mary 54, *54*
Maugham, Harry 58
Maugham, Henry MacDonald
  55, *55,* 56
Maugham, Liza 57, *58-59,* 59
Maugham, Robert Ormond 54
Maugham, Syrie Barnardo
  Wellcome 57, *57,* 58, 73
**Maugham, William
  Somerset** 53, *53, 55,* 60,
  67, 68
  as British intelligence agent
    57, 58, 70, 72, *72,* 73, 75,
    75, 76, *76*
  as editor of *The Venture* 56
  as medical student 56, *56,* 62
  as member of Red Cross
    ambulance unit 57, *57,* 73
  birth 54, *54*

  career 66-68, *66-68*
  characters 64-65, *64-65*
  death 59
  death of parents and 54–55,
    54
  description of self 68
  destruction of letters 59
  divorce 58
  escape from occupied France
    59
  Garrick Club membership
    57
  ill health 55, 58
  in Heidelberg 55, *56*
  in Paris/Spain 56
  key dates 55
  legacy from father 55
  marriage 57
  preface to *Of Human Bondage*
    61
  stammer 54, 55, *55*
  Sunday Express articles 59
  travels 58, *58,* 59, 66-67
  works in outline 69-71,
    69-71
Maupassant, Guy de 8
Melville, Herman 24
'Merle, Madame' of *The
  Portrait of a Lady* 12, 13,
  14, 15, 16, *16,* 19
'Mildred' of *Of Human Bondage*
  61, *61,* 62, *62,* 64, *64*
Millet, Francis Davis 27, *28*
Modern Comedy, A
  (Galsworthy) 92, 93, 94,
  94-95
Modern Utopia, A (Wells) 42
Moon and Sixpence, The
  (Maugham) 57, 58, 66, 68,
  69, *69*
Moore, George 56
Morris, Margaret 81, *81,* 82
Mr Britling Sees it Through
  (Wells) 34
Mrs Craddock (Maugham) 66
Mrs Warren's Profession (Shaw)
  99
Murray, Gilbert 99, 100

N

'Narrator' of *The War of the
  Worlds* 36, 37, *37,* 38, 39,
  39, 40, *40,* 41
Narrow Corner, The
  (Maugham) 67
New Machiavelli, The (Wells)
  33, 43

O

Of Human Bondage (Maugham)
  55, 60-65, *60-65,* 66, 67,
  68, 69

On a Chinese Screen
  (Maugham) 67
On Forsyte 'Change
  (Galsworthy) 93
Orwell, George 52
'Osmond, Gilbert' of *The
  Portrait of a Lady* 13, *13,* 14,
  14, 15, *15,* 16, 17, *17,* 19
Our Betters (Maugham) 57, 58,
  66
Outline of History, The (Wells)
  34, 44

P

Painted Veil, The (Maugham)
  67, 69, 70, *70*
Passionate Friends, The (Wells)
  33
Patrician, The (Galsworthy) 92
Payne, Walter 56
PEN Club 83, *83*
Persse, Jocelyn 10
Pigeon, The (Galsworthy) *82*
Plays Pleasant and Unpleasant
  (Shaw) 98
Poe, Edgar Allan 24, 50
'Polly, Alfred' of *The History of
  Mr Polly* 43, 47
Portrait of a Lady, The (James)
  8, 9, 12-17, *12-17,* 19, 20,
  21, 24
Pound, Ezra 28
'Price, Fanny' of *Of Human
  Bondage* 58, 60, 64
Priestley, J. B. 58
Pygmalion (Shaw) 98, *100*

R

Rain (Maugham) 66, 69, 70, *70*
Razor's Edge, The (Maugham)
  67, 68, 69, 71, *71*
Reeves, Amber 33
Richard, Marthe 74, *74*
Robbins, Amy Catherine
  'Jane' *see* Wells, Amy
  Catherine 'Jane' Robbins
Robinson Crusoe (Defoe) 49
Roosevelt, Franklin Delano 35
Roosevelt, Theodore 35
Rostand, Edmond 49
Royal Court Theatre 92, 96,
  97, *97,* 98, *98*
Ruskin, John 26, *27*

S

Sacred Fount, The (James) 28
'Salvation of Swithin Forsyte,
  The' (Galsworthy) 90, *91*

Sargent, John Singer 10, 25, *26-27*
Sauter, Georg 79
Sauter, Lilian Galsworthy 79, 80
Sauter, Rudolf *78*
science fiction 48-52, *48-52*
Science of Life, The (Wells) 44
Searle, Alan 59, *59*
Secret Agent, The (Conrad) 42
Shape of Things to Come, The (Wells) *35*, 44, *44*
Shaw, George Bernard 10, 33, *33, 43*, 92, 97, 98, *98, 99, 100*
Shelley, Mary 50, 51
Short History of the World (Wells) 44
Silver Box, The (Galsworthy) 80, 92, 94, 96, 98, *99*
Silver Spoon, The (Galsworthy) 94
Small Boy and Others, A (James) 6
Smith-Cumming, Mansfield 73
'Stackpole, Henrietta' of *The Portrait of a Lady* 12, 13, 14, *14*, 16
Stalin, Joseph 35
Steevens, Mrs G. W. 56
Strife (Galsworthy) 92, *92-93*, 94, 99
Summing Up, The (Maugham) 54, 68
Swan Song (Galsworthy) 94
Swift, Jonathan 48, *49*
Swinnerton, Frank 42

T

Tarzan (Burroughs) 52
Temple, Mary 'Minny' 6, 9, *9*
Thackeray, William Makepeace 18

'Theatre of Ideas' 96-100, *96-100*
Threepenny Opera, The (Brecht) *100*
Time Machine, The (Wells) 31, 36, 42, 45, *45*
To Let (Galsworthy) 82, 84
Tolstoy, Leo 18
Tono-Bungay (Wells) 43, 45, 46, *47*
'Touchett, Lydia' of *The Portrait of a Lady* 12, 14, 16, 24
'Touchett, Ralph' of *The Portrait of a Lady* 12, 13, *13*, 14, 15, 16, *16*, 17, 19
'Traitor, The' (Maugham) 73
True History, The (Lucian) 49
Turgenev, Ivan 7, *7*, 8, *9*, 10
Turn of the Screw, The (James) 19, 21, 23, *23*
Twain, Mark 25, *25*
Typee (Melville) 24

U

Uncle Tom's Cabin (Stowe) 100
Unknown, The (Maugham) 58
Unparalleled Adventure of one Hans Pfaall, The (Poe) 50

V

Variations in Flesh Colour and Green: The Balcony (Whistler) *26*
Vedrenne, J. E. 96
Verne, Jules 50, *50*, 51, *51*, 52, *52*
Voyages Extraordinaires (Verne) 50

W

Wallinger, Sir John 57, 73, 74
Walpole, Hugh 6, 10, *67*
War in the Air, The (Wells) 42
War of the Worlds, The (Wells) 31, 35, 36-41, *36-41*, 42, 45, 50
Warburg, Max 75
Washington Square (James) 8, 19, 21, 22, *22*
Waste (Granville-Barker) 99
Wasteland, The (Eliot) 28
Watch and Ward (James) 7
Weld, Mary 19
Wellcome, Henry 57
Wellcome, Syrie *see* Maugham, Syrie Barnado Wellcome
Welles, Orson 35, *35*, 50
Wells, Amy Catherine 'Jane' Robbins 31, 32, *32*, 34, 35, *42*
Wells, Frank (brother of H. G. Wells) 36
Wells, Frank (son of H. G. Wells) 32
Wells, George 32
Wells, Herbert George 29, *29, 30, 32-33*, 38, 48, 49, 50, 51, *51*, 52, *52*
  as propaganda adviser 34
  as teacher 30-31
  at London premiere of *The Shape of Things to Come* 35
  Beerbohm cartoon of *32*
  birth 30
  career 42-44, *42-44*
  characters 40-41, *40-41*
  childhood 30
  children 32
  death 35
  education 30, 31
  epitaph 39
  Fabian Society and 33

  Henry James and 9, 10, *11*, 32, 44
  ill health 31, 34, 35
  jobs, 30, *31*
  key dates 30
  marriage to Isabel 31
  marriage to Jane 31
  nervous breakdown 31-32
  Rebecca West and 33, 34, 35
  self-portrait *43*
  Somerset Maugham and 58
  travels to United States/ Russia 34, *34*, 35
  works in outline 45-47, *45-7*
Wells, Isabel Mary 31, *31, 32*
Wells, Joseph 30, *30*
Wells, Sarah 30, *30, 31, 43*
Wescott, Glenway 57, 58
West, Anthony 33, 34, 35
West, Rebecca 33, *33*, 34, 35
Wharton, Edith 9, 10, *10*
What Maisie Knew (James) 21, 22, *22*
Whistler, James McNeill 25, 26, *26, 27*
White Monkey, The (Galsworthy) 94, *94-95*
Wings of a Dove, The (James) 10, 20
Wiseman, Sir William 75-76
Woolf, Virginia 28
Work, Wealth and Happiness of Mankind, The (Wells) 44
World Set Free, The (Wells) 42
World War I 10, 28, 33, 34, 43-44, 52, 57, 58, 70, 71, 72-76, 82, *82*, 83, 92, 99
World War II *34-35*, 35, 59
'Worlds in the Moon' (Defoe) 49

Z

Zola, Emile 7